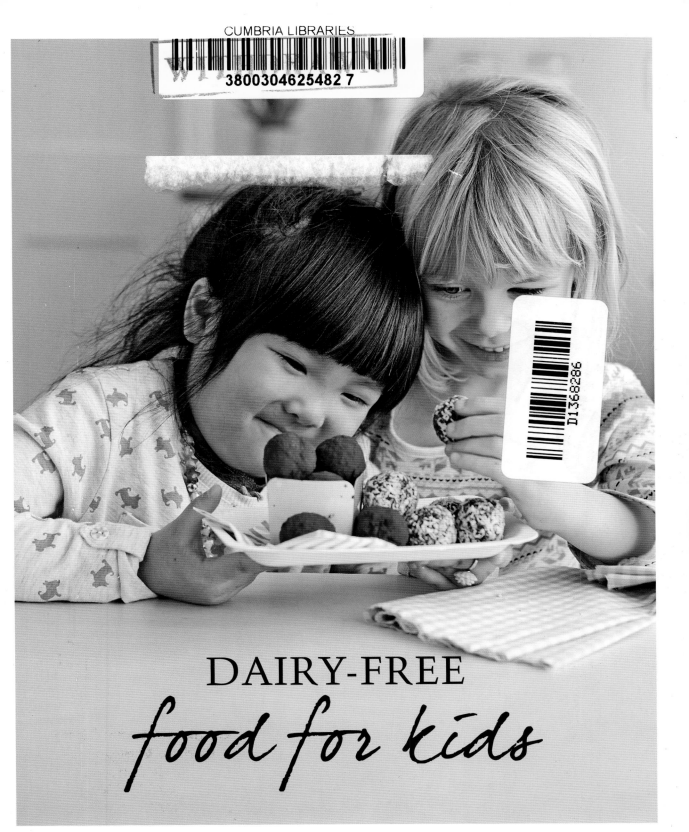

DAIRY-FREE
food for kids

DAIRY-FREE
food for kids

**More than 100 quick & easy recipes
for lactose-intolerant children**

Nicola Graimes

hamlyn

To Ella, Joel and Silvio, with love.

An Hachette UK Company
www.hachette.co.uk

First published in Great Britain in 2015 by
Hamlyn, a division of Octopus Publishing Group Ltd
Carmelite House
50 Victoria Embankment
London EC4Y 0DZ
www.octopusbooks.co.uk

ISBN 978-0-600-63106-4

A CIP catalogue record for this book is available from the British Library.

Printed and bound in China.

10 9 8 7 6 5 4 3 2 1

Both metric and imperial measurements have been given in all recipes. Use one set of measurements only, and not a mixture of both.

Standard level spoon measurements are used in all recipes.
1 tablespoon = one 15 ml spoon
1 teaspoon = one 5 ml spoon

Ovens should be preheated to the specified temperature – if using a fan-assisted oven, follow the manufacturer's instructions for adjusting the time and temperature.

Fresh herbs should be used unless otherwise stated.

Medium eggs should be used unless otherwise stated.

The Department of Health advises that eggs should not be consumed raw. This book contains some dishes made with raw or lightly cooked eggs. It is prudent for vulnerable people such as pregnant and nursing mothers, invalids, the elderly, babies and young children to avoid uncooked or lightly cooked dishes made with eggs. Once prepared, these dishes should be kept refrigerated and used promptly.

This book includes dishes made with nuts and nut derivatives. It is advisable for those with known allergic reactions to nuts and nut derivatives and those who may be potentially vulnerable to these allergies to avoid dishes made with nuts and nut oils. It is also prudent to check the labels of pre-prepared ingredients for the possible inclusion of nut derivatives.

contents

introduction

Introducing kids to healthy eating habits and a positive attitude to food is a really important part of parenting. From initial weaning and moving to solids, to overcoming food fads, food aversions and enjoying a varied and balanced diet, eating habits that are formed during childhood can last a lifetime. But when you have to work around a food allergy or intolerance, it can take a lot more planning and perseverance to lay the groundwork for a healthy approach to – and enjoyment of – food.

Mealtimes have to be thought through in advance and social occasions require careful planning. You will also need to consider the balance between giving your child all the information he or she needs to manage an allergy or intolerance and not allowing it to become a burden or impact upon his or her everyday life more than is absolutely necessary.

We are more aware of cows' milk allergy (CMA) and lactose intolerance these days – symptoms are generally spotted early on and a timely diagnosis of the conditions means that your child won't suffer unduly. You can then introduce alternatives and substitutes that will ensure a well-balanced diet and healthy development.

Allergy or intolerance?

Despite better diagnosis and a greater understanding of food allergies and intolerances, many people still confuse the two and are unsure of the different causes, symptoms and management of each condition. In order to make it easier to differentiate between the two, modern medicine classifies a food allergy as an immune-related condition and a food intolerance as a non-immune-related condition.

This basically means that if your child has CMA, his or her immune system is unable to cope with milk protein and will reject it. Reactions can range from severe diarrhoea, skin complaints and facial swelling to dizziness or anaphylactic shock (although this is a rare reaction). People with CMA will suffer a reaction if they consume even a tiny amount of lactose, which means dairy produce must be completely avoided.

Lactose intolerance is a slightly more forgiving condition in that sufferers may still be able to consume lactose in small quantities and the condition can be managed. We digest lactose (the sugar in milk) with an enzyme called lactase, which breaks down lactose so it can be easily absorbed by the body. Children with lactose intolerance don't produce sufficient lactase, which means the lactose stays in the digestive system and ferments. As with any fermentation process, this produces gas, which is why the symptoms of lactose intolerance include bloating, tummy aches, diarrhoea and wind.

Dairy-free diagnosis

Diagnosing CMA

Most children with CMA develop symptoms very soon after drinking milk or eating dairy produce. This means you will probably link the symptoms to dairy consumption quite early on and you should see your doctor as soon as you have any concerns. A skin prick test (SPT) is the usual way of diagnosing CMA and you should get the results in a matter of minutes. Blood tests are also sometimes required to check for an allergy and you'll have to wait a little longer for definitive results. In the meantime, you might be advised to remove dairy from your child's diet and introduce suitable substitutes. Once a positive diagnosis has been returned, you'll need to see a dietician to discuss your options for alternatives to dairy, and to ensure your child gets all his or her nutritional requirements from other food sources.

Diagnosing lactose intolerance

Lactose intolerance can be trickier to diagnose, as it is a digestive condition. Kids are mini germ factories; they pick up endless tummy complaints, and sickness bugs seem to be on constant rotation around nurseries and schools. However, you might start to notice that your child complains of tummy ache an hour or two after drinking milk or eating diary. If you have your suspicions, make a note of what your child has eaten on the days he or she complains of cramps or pains, or has any other symptoms. Make an appointment with your doctor to discuss your concerns: it's likely it will be recommended that your child avoids dairy for a week or two to see if the symptoms ease.

There are a number of tests available – including a simple breath test and a lactose tolerance test, which checks blood sugar levels after drinking lactose. However, if symptoms disappear once lactose has been removed from the diet, you can be pretty certain that your child is lactose intolerant.

Growing out of allergies

If your child is diagnosed with CMA, you should not assume that this is a life-long condition. The majority of children grow out of CMA by the age of four or five. This means it is very important to get your child tested regularly – this can be done every six months or so. That way, you can readjust your child's diet once he or she has outgrown the condition, and reintroduce dairy. Lactose intolerance, on the other hand, is something your child may have to live with throughout life. If your body doesn't produce sufficient lactase when you are younger, it is unlikely to suddenly start producing it later on in life. Many people actually develop lactose intolerance during adulthood, as the body can diminish its production of lactase with age.

Introducing a dairy-free diet

Once your child has been diagnosed with either CMA or lactose intolerance, you will need to make some fairly fundamental changes to his or her diet. This basically means avoiding all cows' milk drinks and dairy products and replacing these with foods and drinks that will match the nutritional value of dairy. Below is a list of the main dairy foods that should be avoided:

- Milk (including UHT and powdered milk)
- Butter
- Buttermilk
- Cream

Dairy alternatives

So, now that you know the foods to avoid, you'll need to stock up on some alternatives to ensure your child still enjoys a full and varied diet and doesn't miss out on favourite meals and snacks. Milk is the obvious starting point and it's worth checking if your child is intolerant to all animal milk, or just cows' milk. If not, sheep, goat and buffalo milk make good alternatives.

If you must avoid all animal milk, soya milk will be top of your shopping list. It is extremely versatile and is available in sweetened and unsweetened varieties and different flavours. Soya also takes care of dairy-free yogurt, cream and cheese dilemmas and again, these come in different flavours and varieties. Almond, rice, oat and coconut milk are also worth trying.

The health factor

When cutting out a food group from children's diets, it's important to ensure they are getting sufficient vitamins and minerals from other sources. When we think of dairy products, calcium is the first mineral that springs to mind. Essential for bone development and muscle movement, kids also need to keep up their calcium levels in order to avoid medical conditions such as osteoporosis later on in life.

Although it's true that dairy products are a major source of calcium, there are many foods that will help kids to get their recommended 1,000 mg a day (children over nine years need 1,300 mg a day). These are some good sources:

- Tofu
- Almonds
- Sesame seeds
- Tahini
- Spring greens
- Soya beans
- Molasses
- Hazelnuts
- Watercress
- Chickpeas
- Figs
- Parsley
- Leafy green vegetables.

- Cheese (including cream cheese)
- Quark
- Ice cream
- Whey
- Ghee
- Curd
- Whey and whey powder
- Yogurt
- Custard
- Fromage frais.

Check the label

It will be fairly easy to avoid the main culprits but if your child has a serious reaction to dairy, it is vital to check food labels. Dairy products can hide in all kinds of foods, including cereal, bread products, cakes, biscuits, soups, chocolate bars, ready-meals and sauces. It might not be immediately obvious that the food contains a milk product and you'll need to look out for ingredients such as casein (milk protein) and whey protein. You will eventually get to grips with what's lurking deep down in the ingredients list of every pot and package you add to your shopping trolley but, for now, it's a case of carefully checking every label.

confident about the food choices they make. And by showing your child just how delicious a dairy-free diet can be with good home-cooked food they won't feel like they are missing out.

Don't limit your lifestyle

Any dietary conditions that are imposed rather than chosen can be a burden on those who have to follow them. This is especially true for children – at the time in their lives when they should be exploring new ingredients and flavours their diet is suddenly limited, with painful consequences if they step outside the boundaries. However, this also provides opportunities to seek out exciting ingredients that your family might not have tried if it were not for CMA or dairy intolerance. It will encourage you to become more adventurous and creative in the kitchen and your kids will be better informed about their health and wellbeing.

Keep your kids informed

It's all very well for you to know the scientific names of every milk product that could potentially make its way into your larder, but it's equally important that your child is aware of the foods that he or she should avoid. When children are very young you have complete control over their diet. But as soon as they start nursery or school, or get asked to friends' houses for tea, they need an understanding of their condition and to be aware of the foods they can't eat.

Of course, you can talk to the school and other parents to let them know which foods your child should avoid, but it's unrealistic to assume that everyone will remember all of the time. If your child is aware of the foods he or she can't eat from an early age, he or she will be more knowledgeable and confident about telling people about CMA or lactose intolerance when away from home. Make sure adults at play dates, parties and outings have your contact details so they can quickly and easily contact you if your child becomes ill.

The recipes in this book will make life easier, and if you cook them with your child they will learn more about the ingredients they can and can't eat and will become more

About the book

The recipes in this book demonstrate that dairy-free food is exciting, varied and full of flavour. Instead of focusing on the ingredients you have to remove from your child's diet, we celebrate all the incredible ingredients that can be included. There's a selection of snacks, such as Cheesy Popcorn, Crispy Chickpea Bites and Spicy Squash Hummus; quick and easy weekday meals like Chicken Cashew Curry and Salmon and Potato Tortilla; and special dinner ideas for the weekend – everything from Smoked Salmon and Kale Risotto to Thai Tofu Burgers and Sweet and Sour Pork Balls. A selection of puddings and treats makes sure sweet teeth are catered for, and kids will clamour for Peanut Butter and Choc Chip Cookies, Fruity Popsicles, Banana Melts and Chocolate Beetroot Brownies.

Although these recipes have been created with dairy-free diets in mind, they can be enjoyed by the whole family – there's no need to prepare different meals simply because your child has CMA or dairy intolerance. From family gatherings to kids' sleepovers, Saturday film nights to lazy Sunday brunches, these recipes will get kids excited about mealtimes by tucking into nutritious food that doesn't need dairy products to make it work.

breakfast

griddle cakes with apple butter

Serves 4

Preparation time 15 minutes, plus standing

Cooking time 35–40 minutes

200 g (7 oz) self-raising flour

pinch of salt

2 tablespoons caster sugar

300 ml (½ pint) unsweetened dairy-free milk

2 eggs, lightly beaten

sunflower oil or dairy-free spread, for frying

Apple butter

4 dessert apples, peeled, cored and chopped

4 tablespoons water

1 cinnamon stick

½ –1 teaspoon mixed spice, to taste

To serve

maple syrup or honey

dairy-free yogurt

This speedy version of traditional apple butter, which is actually a concentrated fruit spread, is a great alternative to sugary jam. The natural sweetness of the spices means you don't need to add extra sugar to the fruit.

1 Sift the flour and salt into a large bowl, then stir in the sugar and make a well in the centre. Whisk together the milk and eggs in a jug, then pour into the dry ingredients and stir until smooth. Leave to stand for 20 minutes.

2 Meanwhile, make the apple butter. Put the apples in a saucepan with the measurement water and cinnamon stick, cover and cook over a low heat for 20 minutes, stirring frequently and adding a splash more water if necessary, until the apples are very soft and mushy. Remove the cinnamon stick, stir in the mixed spice to taste, then mash with the back of a fork until smooth. Spoon the apple mixture into a ramekin and set aside.

3 Heat a little oil or spread in a large nonstick frying pan over a medium heat, add 3 tablespoons of the batter for each griddle cake and cook for 2 minutes on each side until light golden. Remove from the pan and keep warm in a low oven. Repeat with the remaining batter to make about 16 griddle cakes, adding more oil or spread to the pan as necessary.

4 Top the cakes with the apple butter and a drizzle of maple syrup or honey and serve with yogurt.

banana yogurt crunch

Serves 2

Preparation time 10 minutes, plus cooling

Cooking time 5–6 minutes

30 g (1 oz) jumbo porridge oats

2 tablespoons mixed seeds, such as sunflower, pumpkin and sesame

4 teaspoons maple syrup or honey

200 ml (7 fl oz) dairy-free yogurt, preferably unsweetened

2 small bananas, sliced

1 Put the oats in a large, dry frying pan and toast over a medium-low heat for 3 minutes, stirring occasionally. Add the seeds and cook, stirring, for a further 2–3 minutes until golden.

2 Remove the pan from the heat and stir in the syrup or honey. It will sizzle at first, but keep stirring until the oats and seeds are evenly coated. Leave to cool and crisp up.

3 Divide half of the oat mixture between 2 glasses, then top with half of the yogurt and bananas. Repeat with another layer of the remaining oat mixture, yogurt and bananas.

pineapple & coconut shake

Serves 2

Preparation time 10 minutes

300 g (10 oz) fresh or canned pineapple, drained if necessary, and chopped

200 ml (7 fl oz) coconut drinking milk (*see* page 135 for homemade)

6 tablespoons coconut yogurt

1 teaspoon vanilla extract

½ teaspoon finely grated nutmeg

1 Put the pineapple, coconut milk, yogurt, vanilla extract and three-quarters of the nutmeg in a blender and blend until smooth and creamy.

2 Pour into 2 glasses and sprinkle over the remaining nutmeg.

Tips and tricks

If you can't find coconut yogurt, any dairy-free yogurt would be delicious in this breakfast shake.

spiced hot almond milk

Serves 1

Preparation time 5 minutes, plus infusing

Cooking time 5 minutes

300 ml (½ pint) unsweetened almond milk or other nut milk (*see* page 134 for homemade)

½ cinnamon stick

2 cloves

½ teaspoon vanilla extract

maple syrup, honey or soft brown sugar, to taste

To serve (optional)

ice cubes

freshly grated nutmeg

This version of the popular Spanish drink *horchata* is made with nut milk and flavoured with spices. It makes a comforting, warming drink for any time of the day, but can also be served cold over ice.

1 Pour the milk into a small saucepan, add the cinnamon and cloves and heat gently to almost boiling point, then turn off the heat and leave to infuse for at least 15 minutes, or overnight in the refrigerator.

2 Remove the spices, then stir in the vanilla extract and syrup, honey or sugar to taste. Reheat if serving warm, or serve cold or chilled over ice. Sprinkle over a little nutmeg, if liked.

mixed-grain coconut porridge

Serves 2

Preparation time 5 minutes

Cooking time 7–10 minutes

50 g (2 oz) rolled oats

50 g (2 oz) quinoa, millet or buckwheat flakes

300 ml (½ pint) coconut drinking milk (*see* page 135), plus extra to serve

400 ml (14 fl oz) water

1 teaspoon ground cinnamon

1 ripe banana, mashed

1 tablespoon desiccated coconut, toasted

There are many different types of grain now available and it's worth giving them all a try as they are often super-nutritious.

1 Put the oats and quinoa, millet or buckwheat flakes in a medium-sized saucepan. Pour in the milk and measurement water, then stir in three-quarters of the cinnamon. Bring to the boil, then reduce the heat to low and simmer, part-covered, for 5–8 minutes, stirring frequently, until the grains are tender.

2 Spoon into 2 bowls and top with banana and coconut. Sprinkle over the remaining cinnamon and add extra milk to serve.

blueberry bircher muesli

Serves 2–3

Preparation time 10 minutes, plus overnight soaking

100 g (3½ oz) rolled oats

250 ml (8 fl oz) unsweetened almond milk (*see* page 134), plus extra to serve

3 tablespoons coconut yogurt

1 small dessert apple, cored and grated

2 teaspoons ground flaxseeds (optional)

maple syrup or honey, to taste (optional)

1 tablespoon sunflower seeds, toasted

handful of blueberries

mixed spice, to serve (optional)

This breakfast requires a little pre-planning as the oats need to be soaked overnight.

1 Put the oats in a bowl and pour over the milk. Stir to combine, then cover and leave to soak in the refrigerator overnight.

2 Stir in the yogurt, apple, flaxseeds, if using, and a little syrup or honey to taste, if liked.

3 Spoon into bowls and add a splash of milk if too dry, then top with the sunflower seeds and blueberries. Serve sprinkled with mixed spice, if liked.

eggs arnold bennett

Serves 2

Preparation time 10 minutes

Cooking time 5 minutes

1 tablespoon dairy-free cream cheese

1 tablespoon dairy-free cream

1 teaspoon lemon juice

½ teaspoon finely grated lemon rind

15 g (½ oz) dairy-free spread

3 eggs, lightly beaten

100 g (3½ oz) smoked salmon pieces or
  1 smoked mackerel fillet, skinned and
  flaked into small pieces

pepper

This simplified, dairy-free version of the classic breakfast is topped with smoked salmon or mackerel.

1 Mix together the cream cheese, cream, lemon juice and rind in a bowl and set aside.

2 Heat the spread in a medium-sized, ovenproof frying pan, then pour in the eggs. Turn the pan until the eggs coat the base in an even layer. When the bottom of the omelette is set but the top is still slightly runny, arrange the smoked salmon or mackerel on top, then add the cream cheese mixture in small spoonfuls.

3 Place the pan under a preheated medium-high grill and cook for 2 minutes or until just cooked through. Season with pepper, divide into 2 and serve.

breakfast muffin tortillas

Makes 8

Preparation time 10 minutes

Cooking time 15 minutes

olive oil, for greasing

8 eggs, lightly beaten

3 tablespoons nutritional yeast flakes

2 spring onions, finely chopped

1 cooked, peeled potato, about 225 g (7½ oz), cut into large cubes

3 cooked herby pork or vegetarian sausages, cubed

4 cherry tomatoes, halved

salt and pepper

For convenience, these individual breakfast tortillas are baked in a muffin tray and they also make a handy snack or light lunch.

1 Lightly grease 8 holes of a 12-hole muffin tray with oil.

2 Beat the eggs in a large bowl, then stir in the yeast flakes, spring onions, potato and sausages. Season with salt and pepper.

3 Spoon the mixture evenly into the prepared muffin tray, then place a tomato half on top of each tortilla. Place in a preheated oven, 180°C (350°F), Gas Mark 4, for 15 minutes or until the tortillas are cooked through. Leave to cool in the tin slightly, then turn out and serve.

Tips and tricks
Feel free to adapt the fillings to your liking: ham, spinach, sweetcorn, peas and prawns all make good options.

potato cakes with smoked tofu

Serves 4

Preparation time 20 minutes

Cooking time 25–30 minutes

650 g (1 lb 7 oz) cold cooked, peeled potatoes

40 g (1½ oz) dairy-free spread, melted

50 g (2 oz) plain flour, plus extra for dusting

½ egg, lightly beaten

2 tablespoons olive oil, plus extra for frying

250 g (8 oz) smoked tofu, patted dry and cut into 1 cm (½ inch) cubes

4 large tomatoes, deseeded and quartered

salt and pepper

sweet chilli sauce, to serve (optional)

A perfect way to use up leftover cooked potato, these cakes make a great weekend breakfast-cum-brunch. You also can't beat beans and a poached egg as an alternative to the smoked tofu topping.

1 Grate the cooked potatoes into a large bowl and stir in the spread, flour and beaten egg. Season with salt and pepper, then mix together until combined.

2 Tip the potato mixture on to a floured work surface. Dust the top with more flour and flatten to about 1.5 cm (¾ inch) thick. Stamp out 8 round cakes using a 5 cm (2 inch) plain pastry cutter.

3 Heat enough oil to coat the base of a large frying pan over a medium heat, add the potato cakes and cook, in 2 batches, for 4–5 minutes on each side until golden and cooked through. Reduce the heat slightly if they start to brown too quickly. Remove from the pan and drain on kitchen paper. Keep warm in a low oven while you cook the remaining potato cakes, adding more oil to the pan if necessary.

4 Wipe the pan clean and heat 1 tablespoon of the oil over a medium heat. Add the tofu and fry for 5–8 minutes, turning occasionally, until crisp all over. Remove from the pan and keep warm in the oven while you cook the tomatoes.

5 Heat the remaining oil in the pan, add the tomatoes and cook for 2 minutes until warmed through and starting to soften.

6 Serve the potato cakes topped with the tofu and tomatoes, drizzled with sweet chilli sauce, if liked.

cheesy puff toasts

Serves 1–2

Preparation time 10 minutes

Cooking time 5 minutes

2 slices of wholegrain bread

1 egg, separated

1 teaspoon wholegrain mustard

15 g (½ oz) dairy-free strong Cheddar cheese alternative, grated

1 tablespoon nutritional yeast flakes

To serve

grilled tomatoes

rocket leaves

This savoury soufflé topping for toast is as light as a cloud and so easy to make.

1 Toast 1 side of each slice of bread under a preheated medium-high grill. Meanwhile, mix together the egg yolk, mustard, cheese and yeast flakes in a bowl. In a separate grease-free bowl, whisk the egg white until it forms stiff peaks. Gently fold the egg yolk mixture into the egg white.

2 Remove the toast from the grill and place, toasted-side down, on a plate. Spoon the cheese mixture over each slice of bread, then transfer to the grill and cook for a further 2 minutes or until the tops are puffy and golden.

3 Serve the toasts with grilled tomatoes and rocket leaves.

mexican scrambled eggs

Serves 2

Preparation time 10 minutes

Cooking time 5 minutes

15 g (½ oz) dairy-free spread

3 spring onions, finely chopped

½ red pepper, cored, deseeded and chopped

4 eggs

2 tablespoons unsweetened dairy-free milk

½ teaspoon Mexican spice blend

6 cherry tomatoes, quartered

4 corn taco shells

salt and pepper

To serve (optional)

1 tablespoon chopped fresh coriander

1 small avocado, stoned, peeled and cubed

This breakfast-cum-brunch is a Mexican twist on the classic scrambled egg. Spooned into corn taco shells, the eggs are flavoured with spring onions, red pepper and spices. Soft flour tortillas or even toast make good alternatives to the tacos, if you prefer.

1 Heat the spread in a frying pan over a medium heat, add the spring onions and red pepper and fry for 2 minutes.

2 Mix together the eggs, milk and spice blend in a bowl and season with salt and pepper to taste.

3 Pour the egg mixture into the pan, reduce the heat to medium-low and cook gently, stirring and folding the egg until scrambled. Just before the eggs are cooked, stir in the tomatoes to warm through.

4 Meanwhile, stand the taco shells on a baking sheet and place in a preheated oven, 180°C (350°F), Gas Mark 4, for 2–3 minutes until warmed through.

5 Spoon the scrambled egg mixture into the taco shells. Scatter the coriander and avocado over the top, if using, and serve.

snacks

crispy chickpea bites

Serves 4

Preparation time 5 minutes

Cooking time 35–45 minutes

400 g (13 oz) can chickpeas, rinsed and drained

1 tablespoon olive oil or melted coconut oil

2 teaspoons Cajun spice mix or other spice blend

salt

1 Line a plate with kitchen paper, tip the chickpeas on top and pat dry with a second sheet of paper.

2 Transfer the chickpeas to a bowl and stir in the oil, the spice mix and a large pinch of salt until thoroughly combined and evenly coated.

3 Spread the chickpeas on a baking tray and place in a preheated oven, 180°C (350°F), Gas Mark 4, for 35–45 minutes, turning occasionally, until crisp and golden. Leave to cool before serving in paper cones. Store in an airtight container for up to 1 week.

seasoned popcorn

Serves 4

Preparation time 5 minutes

Cooking time 8 minutes

1½ tablespoons sunflower oil

100 g (3½ oz) popping corn

1 tablespoon nutritional yeast flakes

2 teaspoons smoked paprika or
dried chives

A useful standby when a snack is called for!

1 Heat the oil in a large saucepan with a tight-fitting lid. Add the corn, cover and heat until it starts to pop. Shake the pan occasionally and continue to cook until the popping stops.

2 Once all the corn has popped, tip it into a large bowl, add the yeast flakes and paprika or chives and turn the popcorn until it is coated in the flavourings. Serve immediately.

honey-soy nuts & seeds

Serves 4

Preparation time 5 minutes

Cooking time 8–10 minutes

200 g (7 oz) unsalted nuts and seeds,
such as almonds, cashews, pistachios,
hazelnuts, sunflower seeds and pumpkin
seeds (nuts and seeds kept separate)

1 tablespoon reduced-salt soy sauce

1 teaspoon clear honey

A handful of nuts and seeds make a nutritious snack. These are flavoured with a delicious combination of runny honey and soy sauce.

1 Place the nuts in a baking tray and roast in a preheated oven, 160°C (325°F), Gas Mark 3, for 6 minutes.

2 Add the seeds to the tray and turn until combined, then roast for a further 2–4 minutes until they smell toasted and start to colour. (Keep an eye on them as they can burn easily.)

3 Transfer the nuts and seeds to a bowl, spoon over the soy sauce and honey and turn with a spoon until well coated. Leave to cool before serving. Store in an airtight container for up to 1 week.

cheesy tomato toasts

Serves 2

Preparation time 10 minutes

Cooking time 10 minutes

2 slices of seeded wholemeal bread

1 egg yolk

1 teaspoon Dijon mustard

few drops of Worcestershire sauce

1 tablespoon dairy-free cream cheese

1 teaspoon nutritional yeast flakes

1 tablespoon dairy-free spread

1 tablespoon plain flour

4 tablespoons unsweetened
  dairy-free milk

4 cherry tomatoes, each cut into 6

carrot and celery sticks, to serve
  (optional)

Fans of regular cheese on toast won't be disappointed with this dairy-free alternative.

1 Toast 1 side of each slice of bread under a preheated hot grill. Transfer to a board, toasted-side down. Meanwhile, beat together the egg yolk, mustard, Worcestershire sauce, cream cheese and yeast flakes in a bowl, then set aside.

2 Melt the spread in a small saucepan, then whisk in the flour and cook over a low heat for 1 minute until it forms a light golden paste. Add the egg yolk mixture and heat through briefly, whisking continuously. Remove the pan from the heat, then stir in the milk. Return to a low heat and cook for a few minutes, stirring continuously, until it forms a smooth, thick sauce.

3 Spoon the mixture over each slice of bread. Arrange the tomatoes on top and grill for 2–3 minutes until the tomatoes start to colour. Serve with carrot and celery sticks, if liked.

satay dip with pitta crisps

Serves 4–6

Preparation time 10 minutes

Cooking time 20 minutes

Satay dip

4 tablespoons peanut butter

1 garlic clove, crushed

1 tablespoon reduced-salt soy sauce

1 tablespoon hoisin sauce

1 tablespoon sesame oil

1 teaspoon soft light brown sugar
  or honey

¼ teaspoon dried chilli flakes (optional)

juice of ½ lime

50 ml (2 fl oz) coconut drinking milk
  (*see* page 135 for homemade)

100 ml (3½ fl oz) water

Pitta crisps

4 pitta breads

olive oil, for brushing

Perfect for dunking fresh vegetables or slices of crisp pitta bread into, this Asian peanut dip can also be used as a sauce for noodles or rice.

1 Make the pitta crisps. Slice down the sides of each pitta bread to open them out, then lightly brush both sides with olive oil. Place 1 pitta in a large, dry frying pan and toast for about 5 minutes, turning once, until crisp and golden. Remove from the pan and leave to cool. Repeat with the remaining pittas.

2 Meanwhile, put all the dip ingredients in a small saucepan and heat gently, stirring, until warmed through and thickened.

3 Break the pittas into large pieces and serve with the satay dip.

easy mushroom spread

Serves 4–6

Preparation time 15 minutes, plus soaking

Cooking time 20 minutes

10 g (½ oz) dried porcini mushrooms

40 g (1½ oz) dairy-free spread

1 tablespoon olive oil

1 onion, finely chopped

250 g (8 oz) chestnut mushrooms, finely chopped

½ teaspoon dried thyme

2 garlic cloves, finely chopped

3 tablespoons dairy-free cream cheese

salt and pepper

toast, pitta bread or crackers, to serve

1 Put the porcini in a heatproof bowl, cover with just-boiled water and leave to soak for 20 minutes until softened. Drain the mushrooms, reserving the soaking liquid, and finely chop.

2 Meanwhile, heat the spread and oil in a large frying pan over a medium heat, add the onion and cook for 8 minutes, stirring frequently, until softened. Add the soaked porcini, chestnut mushrooms and thyme and cook for a further 10 minutes until very soft and any liquid from the mushrooms has evaporated. Stir in the garlic, then leave to cool slightly.

3 Tip the mushroom mixture into a food processor or blender with the cream cheese, season and blend until smooth.

4 Spoon the mixture into a bowl and serve immediately, spread over toast, pitta or crackers. Alternatively, cover and store in the refrigerator for up to 5 days.

smoked salmon pâté

Serves 4

Preparation time 10 minutes

100 g (3½ oz) smoked salmon pieces

125 g (4 oz) dairy-free cream cheese

2 tablespoons soya cream, plus extra if needed

juice of ½ lemon

1 tablespoon snipped chives

pepper

toast, pitta breads or crackers, to serve

The creamy texture of this pâté makes it ideal for kids that are wary of fishy dishes.

1 Put the smoked salmon, cream cheese, cream, lemon juice and chives in a food processor or blender. Season with pepper and blend to an almost smooth pâté, adding a little extra cream if necessary.

2 Spoon the pâté into a bowl and serve with fingers of toast, pitta breads or crackers.

tuna cucumber cups

Serves 2

Preparation time 10 minutes

100 g (3½ oz) canned tuna in spring
  water, drained

1 teaspoon reduced-salt soy sauce

½ teaspoon sesame oil

1 spring onion, finely chopped

15 cm (6 inch) piece of cucumber

2 teaspoons sesame seeds, toasted

Thick, round slices of cucumber make the
perfect 'cup', ready to be filled, once the
central seeds are scooped out.

1 Mix together the tuna, soy sauce, sesame oil and spring
onion in a bowl.

2 Cut the cucumber into 2.5 cm (1 inch) thick slices. Using a
teaspoon, scoop the seeds out of each slice to form cup shapes,
leaving the bases intact.

3 Spoon the tuna mixture into the cups and sprinkle with
sesame seeds before serving.

Tips and tricks
In this recipe the cucumber is stuffed with an
Asian tuna mix, but the popular combination
of tuna, sweetcorn, spring onion and mayo
would also work well.

spicy squash hummus

Serves 4–6

Preparation time 15 minutes

Cooking time 30 minutes

475 g (15 oz) butternut squash, peeled, deseeded and cut into bite-sized chunks

2 tablespoons extra virgin olive oil, plus extra to serve

1 teaspoon ground allspice (optional)

5 tablespoons dairy-free yogurt, preferably unsweetened

2 tablespoons light tahini

1 garlic clove, crushed

juice of 1 lemon

1 teaspoon sesame seeds, toasted

salt and pepper

Tahini is a calcium-rich sesame seed paste and makes a great addition to a dairy-free diet. It adds a slightly nutty flavour and creamy texture to soups, stews, dips and sauces as well as this delicious hummus.

1 Place the squash, half the olive oil and the allspice, if using, in a bowl and toss until the squash is well coated, then tip on to a baking sheet. Place in a preheated oven, 190°C (375°F), Gas Mark 5, for 30 minutes, turning once, until tender and starting to colour in places. Leave to cool for 5 minutes.

2 Transfer the squash to a food processor or blender, add the yogurt, tahini, garlic, lemon juice and the remaining olive oil. Season, then blend until smooth. Alternatively, tip the squash and other ingredients into a bowl and mash with a potato masher or the back of a fork. Add a little warm water if the mixture is too thick.

3 Spoon the hummus into a serving bowl, sprinkle with the sesame seeds and drizzle over a little extra oil before serving.

cashew cheese balls

Serves 4

**Preparation time 20 minutes,
  plus soaking**

175 g (6 oz) cashew nuts

100 ml (3½ fl oz) cold water

1 garlic clove, crushed

2 teaspoons lemon juice

5 tablespoons shelled unsalted
  pistachio nuts or other nuts or seeds,
  coarsely ground

5 tablespoons finely chopped mixed
  herbs, such as oregano, chives
  and parsley

salt and pepper

toast, rice cakes or crackers, to serve

1 Put the cashews in a heatproof bowl, cover with hot water and leave to soak for at least 2 hours or overnight, if possible.

2 Drain the nuts, discarding the soaking water. Tip into a food processor or blender, add the measurement water and blend to a coarse paste, scraping down the sides of the jug if necessary. Transfer to a bowl, season with salt and pepper and stir in the garlic and lemon juice.

3 Place the ground pistachios and mixed herbs on separate plates. Shape 1 tablespoon of the cashew cheese into a ball, then roll in the pistachios until evenly coated. Form a second ball, then roll it in the herbs. Repeat with the remaining cashew cheese, rolling half of the balls in the nuts and half in the herbs. Transfer the coated balls to a plate, cover and chill to firm up slightly. Serve with toast, rice cakes or crackers.

quesadillas

Serves 2

Preparation time 8 minutes

Cooking time 9–10 minutes

2 bacon rashers

2 tablespoons dairy-free cream cheese

2 large white or seeded tortillas

¼ red onion, thinly sliced

1 tomato, sliced

handful of rocket or watercress leaves

olive oil, for frying

Filled with a delicious combination of bacon, red onion, tomato and dairy-free cream cheese, this tortilla 'sandwich' makes a quick, tasty snack. Leave it to stand for a couple of minutes after cooking to allow the filling to cool and firm up slightly, otherwise it's in danger of running out when you cut into it.

1 Cook the bacon over a foil-lined grill pan under a preheated hot grill until cooked, turning once, then drain on kitchen paper. Cut into pieces and leave to one side.

2 Spread 1 tablespoon of the cream cheese over each tortilla. Arrange the onion, tomato, bacon and rocket or watercress over 1 tortilla, then top with the remaining tortilla, cream cheese-side down.

3 Drizzle a little oil over the base of a large frying pan and heat over a medium heat. Place the quesadilla in the pan, press the edges down slightly so the filling doesn't escape and cook for 2–3 minutes or until golden and starting to crisp. Carefully turn the quesadilla over using a spatula and cook for a further 2 minutes until golden.

4 Slide the quesadilla out of the pan on to a serving plate and leave to cool for a few minutes. Cut into wedges and serve with rocket or watercress leaves.

socca pizza

Serves 6–8

Preparation time 15 minutes,
  plus standing

Cooking time 15–20 minutes

200 g (7 oz) gram flour

1 teaspoon baking powder

½ teaspoon salt

450 ml (¾ pint) lukewarm water

4 tablespoons extra virgin olive oil

1 small red onion, sliced into rings

75 g (3 oz) sliced salami or chorizo

10 cherry tomatoes, halved

50 g (2 oz) dairy-free herb and garlic
  cream cheese or 100 g (3½ oz)
  dairy-free mozzarella cheese
  alternative, sliced into chunks

This is a popular street food in Italy that is dairy-free and made with gluten-free gram flour. It can loosely be described as a type of pancake and comes topped with slices of salami, cherry tomatoes, red onion and dairy-free cheese, but feel free to add your own favourite toppings.

1 Mix together the gram flour, baking powder and salt in a large bowl and make a well in the centre. Gradually pour the measurement water and half the olive oil into the dry ingredients, whisking continuously to form a light batter. Cover and leave to stand for 2 hours or overnight in the refrigerator.

2 Pour the remaining olive oil into a 30 x 25 cm (12 x 10 inch) baking tray and place in a preheated oven, 220°C (425°F) Gas Mark 7, for 5 minutes until very hot.

3 Carefully remove the baking tray from the oven and pour the batter into the tray. Scatter the red onion, salami or chorizo and tomatoes over the top, then add teaspoonfuls of the cream cheese or the mozzarella chunks. Bake for 15–20 minutes until set and golden around the edges. Leave to stand for a couple of minutes before cutting into wedges.

cheesy corn muffins

Makes 6

Preparation time 15 minutes

Cooking time 20 minutes

50 g (2 oz) dairy-free spread, melted, plus extra for greasing

100 g (3½ oz) instant polenta or cornmeal

40 g (1½ oz) plain flour

1 teaspoon baking powder

½ teaspoon bicarbonate of soda

½ teaspoon salt

1 teaspoon English mustard powder

1 large egg, lightly beaten

6 tablespoons dairy-free yogurt

7 tablespoons unsweetened dairy-free milk

½ red pepper, cored, deseeded and diced

50 g (2 oz) dairy-free strong Cheddar cheese alternative, grated

1 Lightly grease a 6-hole muffin tray.

2 Mix together the polenta, flour, baking powder, bicarbonate of soda, salt and mustard powder in a bowl. Whisk together the egg, yogurt, milk and melted spread in a jug, then pour into the dry ingredients and add the red pepper and cheese. Using a wooden spoon, stir together until just combined.

3 Spoon the mixture evenly into the prepared muffin tray and smooth the tops. Place in a preheated oven, 190°C (375°F), Gas Mark 5, for 20 minutes until risen and a skewer inserted into the centres comes out clean. Transfer to a wire rack to cool. Serve warm or cold.

date & nut snack balls

Makes 12

Preparation time 15 minutes, plus chilling

50 g (2 oz) cashew nuts

50 g (2 oz) hazelnuts

1 tablespoon sunflower seeds

finely grated rind of 1 orange

3 tablespoons orange juice

100 g (3½ oz) ready-to-eat dried dates

1 heaped tablespoon cocoa powder,
  plus extra for dusting

3 tablespoons desiccated coconut

These are just the thing when only something sweet will do… The bite-sized snack balls are packed with nutritious, energy-sustaining nuts, seeds and fruit.

1 Place the nuts and seeds in a food processor and grind to a coarse powder. Tip the mixture into a bowl and stir in the orange rind.

2 Put the orange juice and dates in the processor and blend to a purée, scraping down the sides of the jug if necessary. Add the date mixture to the ground nuts and seeds, then stir in the cocoa powder and combine to form a coarse paste.

3 Place some extra cocoa powder and the coconut on separate plates. Shape the date mixture into 12 walnut-sized balls, then roll half in the cocoa powder and half in the coconut until they are all evenly coated.

4 Transfer the balls to a plate, cover and chill for 1 hour before serving. Store in an airtight container in the refrigerator for up to 1 week.

Tips and tricks
You could use raw cacao powder instead of the cocoa, if you can find it.

weekdays

creamy tomato & lentil soup

Serves 4

Preparation time 15 minutes

Cooking time 30 minutes

1 tablespoon extra virgin olive oil

1 large onion, chopped

2 carrots, sliced

1 celery stick, sliced

100 g (3½ oz) split red lentils, rinsed

2 bay leaves

680 g (1½ lb) jar passata

600 ml (1 pint) vegetable stock, plus extra if needed (optional)

1 teaspoon dried oregano

½ teaspoon Worcestershire sauce

3 tablespoons oat cream or other dairy-free cream

salt and pepper

To serve

crispy fried onions

nutritional yeast flakes

This creamy and filling main meal soup is puréed until smooth, with not a lentil or vegetable in sight! Serve it with crusty bread.

1 Heat the oil in a large saucepan over a medium heat, add the onion, carrots and celery, cover and sauté for 7 minutes until softened, stirring occasionally to prevent the vegetables sticking to the bottom of the pan.

2 Stir in the lentils and bay leaves, then the passata, stock and oregano and bring to the boil. Reduce the heat to low, cover and simmer for 20 minutes or until the vegetables and lentils are tender.

3 Using a stick blender, blend the soup until smooth. Stir in the Worcestershire sauce and season to taste. Add the oat cream and a little extra stock or water if necessary.

4 Ladle into bowls and serve sprinkled with crispy fried onions and yeast flakes.

carrot pancakes

Serves 4

**Preparation time 20 minutes,
  plus standing**

Cooking time 12 minutes

500 g (1 lb) carrots, coarsely grated

3 spring onions, finely chopped

2 large handfuls of coriander leaves,
  chopped

75 g (3 oz) gram flour, sifted

8 eggs

sunflower oil, for frying

salt and pepper

To serve

1 recipe quantity Dairy-free Tzatziki
  (*see* page 136)

rocket leaves (optional)

1 Combine the carrots, spring onions and coriander in a bowl with the gram flour. Beat 4 of the eggs in a jug, season and add to the carrot mixture. Stir, then let stand for 10 minutes.

2 Heat enough oil to coat the base of a large frying pan over a medium heat, add 4 large dessertspoonfuls of the batter to make 4 pancakes, flattening each with a spatula until about 8 cm (3¼ inches) across, and cook for 2 minutes on each side or until set and golden. Remove from the pan, blot on a kitchen paper and keep warm in a low oven. Repeat with the remaining batter to make 12 pancakes.

3 Meanwhile, bring a large sauté pan of water to a simmer. Break 1 of the remaining eggs into a cup. Swirl the water and slip the egg into the pan, then repeat with the remaining eggs. Simmer, occasionally spooning the water over the top of the eggs, until the whites are set but the yolks remain runny.

4 Top each serving of pancakes with a poached egg and a few spoonfuls of the tzatziki. Serve with rocket leaves, if liked.

haddock & sweetcorn chowder

Serves 4

Preparation time 20 minutes

Cooking time 20 minutes

15 g (½ oz) dairy-free spread

1 tablespoon olive oil

1 large onion, chopped

1 large celery stick, thinly sliced

1 large carrot, cut into large cubes

1 large leek, trimmed, cleaned and sliced

450 g (14½ oz) undyed smoked
   haddock fillet

1 fish stock cube

2 bay leaves

625 g (1 lb 6 oz) potatoes, peeled and
   cut into bite-sized cubes

200 g (7 oz) sweetcorn kernels

200 ml (7 fl oz) unsweetened
   dairy-free milk

4 tablespoons dairy-free cream cheese

handful of parsley leaves, chopped

salt and pepper

crusty bread, to serve

Soups make a perfect warming, filling midweek meal. Stir in the dairy-free cream cheese right at the end to prevent it curdling in the heat of the soup.

1 Heat the spread and oil in a large heavy-based saucepan over a medium heat, add the onion, celery, carrot and leek and sauté for 5 minutes, stirring frequently, until softened.

2 Meanwhile, put the haddock in a large sauté or frying pan and pour over enough water to cover. Bring almost to the boil, then turn off the heat and leave to stand for 3–5 minutes until the haddock is just cooked through. Using a fish slice, remove the haddock from the pan and leave to cool slightly.

3 Strain the fish cooking water into a jug and pour in extra hot water, if necessary, to make it up to 900 ml (1½ pints). Stir in the fish stock cube until dissolved.

4 Add the bay leaves to the sautéed vegetables, pour in the fish stock and bring to the boil, then add the potatoes. Reduce the heat and simmer for 10 minutes until the potatoes are almost tender.

5 Meanwhile, remove the skin and any bones from the haddock and flake the fish into large pieces.

6 Add the sweetcorn and milk to the potatoes and simmer for 3 minutes. Add the haddock and cook for a further 2 minutes until the fish is heated through, then season.

7 Remove the pan from the heat and stir in the cream cheese and parsley. Ladle into large bowls and serve with crusty bread.

refried bean tacos

Serves 4

Preparation time 20 minutes

Cooking time 10 minutes

400 g (13 oz) can kidney beans in chilli sauce

400 g (13 oz) can kidney beans, rinsed and drained

1 small red onion, sliced

1 large garlic clove, sliced

1 tablespoon olive oil

1 teaspoon smoked paprika

1 teaspoon dried oregano

8 corn taco shells

shredded crisp lettuce

2 tomatoes, diced

mixed salad, to serve

Guacamole

2 avocadoes, halved, stoned, peeled and sliced

1 large garlic clove, crushed

juice of 1 lime

salt and pepper

Homemade refried beans are quick and easy to make, so are ideal for a weekday meal. Simply serve them with a mixed salad.

1 Mash together all the guacamole ingredients using the back of a fork until smooth. Season to taste, cover and set aside.

2 Put the kidney beans in chilli sauce, half the drained kidney beans, the red onion and garlic in a food processor or blender and blend together until almost smooth. Transfer the mixture to a large frying pan with the remaining kidney beans, olive oil, paprika and oregano. Season and heat through for 5–7 minutes, stirring frequently and adding a splash of water if necessary.

3 Meanwhile, stand the taco shells on a baking sheet and place in a preheated oven, 180°C (350°F), Gas Mark 4, for 2–3 minutes until warmed through.

4 Spoon a little shredded lettuce into each taco, then top with the bean mixture and a good spoonful of guacamole. Scatter over the tomato and serve with a mixed salad.

chicken cashew curry

Serves 4

Preparation time 20 minutes

Cooking time 30 minutes

75 g (3 oz) unsalted cashew nuts

300 ml (½ pint) water

1 tablespoon sunflower oil

1 onion, finely chopped

3 garlic cloves, crushed

3.5 cm (1½ inch) piece of fresh root ginger, peeled and finely grated

1 teaspoon ground cumin

2 teaspoons ground coriander

1 teaspoon turmeric

1 tablespoon garam masala

½ teaspoon mild chilli powder, or to taste (optional)

500 g (1 lb) boneless, skinless chicken breasts, cut into large chunks

4 tablespoons dairy-free yogurt, preferably unsweetened

salt and pepper

To serve

10 cherry tomatoes, quartered

handful of fresh coriander, chopped

cooked brown basmati rice

1 Put the cashews in a large, dry frying pan and toast over a medium-low heat for 5 minutes, turning once, until golden. Remove from the heat and leave to cool. Tip the nuts into a grinder or mini food processor with 100 ml (3½ fl oz) of the measurement water and blend to a smooth paste.

2 Heat the oil in a saucepan over a medium-low heat, add the onion, cover and cook for 8 minutes, stirring occasionally, until soft. Add the garlic and ginger and cook for a further 1 minute.

3 Stir in the spices, ground cashews and remaining measurement water and bring to the boil. Add the chicken, then reduce the heat and simmer, part-covered, for 15 minutes or until the chicken is cooked through and the sauce has reduced and thickened. Season to taste and stir in the yogurt. Top with the tomatoes and coriander and serve with rice.

lentil & squash dhal

Serves 4

Preparation time 15 minutes

Cooking time 30 minutes

2 tablespoons sunflower oil or coconut oil

1 large onion, diced

2 large garlic cloves, finely chopped

2.5 cm (1 inch) piece of unpeeled fresh root ginger, grated

175 g (6 oz) peeled and deseeded butternut squash, cut into bite-sized chunks

125 g (4 oz) split red lentils, rinsed

600 ml (1 pint) water

2 heaped tablespoons mild curry paste

1 teaspoon turmeric

½ teaspoon dried chilli flakes (optional)

100 ml (3½ fl oz) canned coconut milk

salt and pepper

To serve

4 large hard-boiled eggs, shelled and halved

4 tablespoons Dairy-free Raita (*see* page 136)

wholemeal chapattis, warmed, or brown basmati rice

This is a great introduction to curry as it is mildly spiced yet still full of flavour. The coconut milk also helps to temper the heat from the spices as well as add a delicious creaminess. It can be served on its own with Indian breads or topped with a hard-boiled egg.

1 Heat the oil in a large heavy-based saucepan over a medium heat, add the onion, cover and cook for 8 minutes, stirring occasionally, until softened. Add the garlic, ginger and squash, then stir in the lentils and measurement water.

2 Bring to the boil, then reduce the heat and stir in the curry paste, turmeric and chilli flakes, if using. Simmer, part-covered, for 20 minutes or until the squash and lentils are tender.

3 Using a stick blender, blend the dhal until smooth, then stir in the coconut milk, season to taste and reheat briefly.

4 Spoon the dhal into large serving bowls and top each portion with a hard-boiled egg and some raita. Serve with warm chapattis or rice.

turkey burritos

Serves 4

Preparation time 20 minutes

Cooking time 25–30 minutes

175 g (6 oz) brown basmati rice

1 teaspoon turmeric

1 tablespoon olive oil

2 red onions, sliced

2 garlic cloves, chopped

400 g (13 oz) can chopped tomatoes

400 g (13 oz) can kidney beans, rinsed and drained

200 ml (7 fl oz) water

1 teaspoon ground coriander

1 teaspoon ground cumin

1 teaspoon smoked paprika

400 g (13 oz) ready-cooked turkey, cut into long strips

To serve

4 large soft tortillas

75 g (3 oz) dairy-free strong Cheddar cheese alternative, grated

1 recipe quantity Guacamole (*see* page 45)

mixed salad

Making these delicious burritos is an excellent way of using up leftover cooked meat, such as turkey, chicken, pork and beef, from the Sunday roast.

1 Put the rice in a saucepan and add enough water to cover by 1.5 cm (¾ inch). Stir in the turmeric and bring to the boil, then reduce the heat to its lowest setting, cover and simmer for 20–25 minutes until the rice is tender and the water has been absorbed. Turn off the heat and leave the rice to stand for 5 minutes.

2 Meanwhile, heat the oil in a separate large heavy-based saucepan and cook three-quarters of the onions for 6 minutes until softened. Stir in the garlic and cook for a further 1 minute.

3 Add the tomatoes, kidney beans and measurement water and bring to the boil. Reduce the heat, stir in the spices and cook, part-covered, for 15 minutes until the sauce has reduced and thickened. Stir in the turkey and heat through until piping hot.

4 To serve, warm the tortillas, 2 at a time, in a large, dry frying pan. Place a few spoonfuls of the rice on each tortilla and top with the sauce. Finally, top with the cheese, the remaining red onion and a spoonful of guacamole. Fold the tortilla over the filling and serve with the remaining rice and a mixed salad.

Tips and tricks

For vegetarians, aubergines, tofu or mushrooms would work well in place of turkey.

ham fritters with salsa

Serves 4

Preparation time 15 minutes

Cooking time 25 minutes

250 g (8 oz) sweetcorn kernels

3 slices of thickly cut, good-quality cured ham, about 250 g (8 oz) total weight, diced

175 g (6 oz) cooked rice

60 g (2¼ oz) plain flour

2 eggs, lightly beaten

75 ml (3 fl oz) unsweetened dairy-free milk

sunflower oil, for frying

Pineapple salsa

½ small pineapple, skinned, cored and diced

½ red onion, diced

1 red chilli, deseeded and diced (optional)

juice of ½ lime

handful of coriander leaves, chopped

salt and pepper

1 Mix together all the salsa ingredients in a bowl, season with salt and pepper and set aside.

2 Put the corn kernels, ham, cooked rice and flour in a large bowl and mix together. Whisk together the eggs and milk in a jug, then pour into the corn mixture and stir until combined.

3 Heat enough oil to coat the base of a large frying pan over a medium heat, drop in 4 large dessertspoonfuls of the mixture to make 4 fritters and cook for 3 minutes on each side or until set and lightly golden. Remove from the pan, drain on kitchen paper and keep warm in a low oven. Repeat with the remaining mixture to make 16 fritters.

4 Serve the fritters with the pineapple salsa.

sesame chicken nuggets

Serves 4

Preparation time 15 minutes,
   plus marinating

Cooking time 20 minutes

4 tablespoons reduced-salt soy sauce

2 tablespoons honey

2 tablespoons sesame oil

600 g (1¼ lb) mini chicken breast fillets

olive oil, for greasing

225 g (7½ oz) sesame seeds

Chilli-mayo dip

6 tablespoons dairy-free mayonnaise

3 tablespoons sweet chilli sauce

1 tablespoon lemon juice

To serve (optional)

roasted sweet potato chips

steamed sliced carrots

A healthier version of ever-popular chicken nuggets, these are coated in calcium-rich sesame seeds and then baked in the oven until crisp and golden. The nuggets can be served with sweet potato wedges and favourite vegetables, or with a vegetable noodle stir-fry.

1 Mix together the soy sauce, honey and sesame oil in a large, shallow dish. Add the chicken and turn to coat in the marinade, then cover and leave to marinate in the refrigerator for at least 30 minutes.

2 Lightly oil 2 large baking trays. Put the sesame seeds on a large plate and roll each chicken fillet in the sesame seeds until evenly coated, then transfer to the prepared baking trays.

3 Place in a preheated oven, 180°C (350°F), Gas Mark 4, for 20 minutes, turning once, until the chicken is cooked through and the seeds are golden.

4 Meanwhile, mix together all the chilli-mayo dip ingredients in a bowl.

5 Serve the chicken nuggets with the chilli-mayo dip and accompanied by roasted sweet potato chips and sliced steamed carrots, if liked.

love-it linguine

Serves 4

Preparation time 5 minutes

Cooking time 15 minutes

400 g (13 oz) dried linguine pasta

50 g (2 oz) dairy-free spread

4 teaspoons yeast extract

4 heaped teaspoons nutritional
  yeast flakes

pepper

2 tablespoons toasted pine nuts,
  to serve

This pasta dish is so quick to make it could be served as an after-school snack as well as a speedy supper.

1 Cook the pasta in a large saucepan of boiling water according to the packet instructions until al dente. Drain, reserving 100 ml (3½ fl oz) of the cooking water.

2 Return the pasta to the pan with half of the reserved cooking water and place on the still-warm hob. Add the spread, yeast extract and yeast flakes and toss until combined, adding more of the cooking water to loosen the pasta if necessary. Season with pepper and serve sprinkled with pine nuts.

Tips and tricks
Serve the linguine topped with a fried egg and, of course, lots of veg for a more substantial meal.

tomato pesto orzo

Serves 4

Preparation time 15 minutes,
  plus soaking

Cooking time 25 minutes

100 g (3½ oz) sun-dried tomatoes

2 red peppers, cored, deseeded and
  cut into long wedges

100 ml (3½ fl oz) extra virgin olive oil,
  plus extra for brushing

75 g (3 oz) cashew nuts

2 garlic cloves, crushed

375 g (12 oz) dried orzo pasta

salt and pepper

handful of basil leaves, torn, to garnish

1 Place the sun-dried tomatoes in a heatproof bowl, cover with just-boiled water and soak for 30 minutes until softened.

2 Meanwhile, lightly brush both sides of the peppers with oil and cook under a preheated hot grill for 15 minutes, turning once, until softened and the skins have started to blacken. Put the peppers in a bowl, cover with clingfilm and leave until cool enough to handle; this will make the peppers easier to peel.

3 While the peppers are grilling, put the cashews in a large, dry frying pan and toast over a medium-low heat for 5 minutes, tossing the pan occasionally, until the cashews smell toasted and start to colour. Tip the nuts into a bowl and leave to cool, then roughly chop.

4 Peel the skins off the peppers and discard. Drain the tomatoes, reserving the soaking water. Put the tomatoes in a food processor or a blender with the peppers, 100 ml (3½ fl oz) of the soaking liquid and the oil, then blend until smooth. Tip the tomato mixture into a bowl with 50 g (2 oz) of the cashews and the garlic, season to taste and stir until combined. Set aside.

5 Cook the pasta in a large saucepan of boiling water according to the packet instructions. Drain, reserving 75 ml (3 fl oz) of the cooking water.

6 Return the pasta to the pan and spoon in enough of the pesto to coat. Add the pasta cooking water to loosen the sauce and toss until combined. Serve sprinkled with the remaining cashews and the basil leaves. Store any leftover pesto in a sealable jar in the refrigerator for up to 10 days.

creamy tomato & tuna pasta

Serves 4

Preparation time 15 minutes

Cooking time 15 minutes

2 large garlic cloves, chopped

1 tablespoon olive oil

400 g (13 oz) can chopped tomatoes

100 ml (3½ fl oz) water

1 tablespoon tomato ketchup

75 g (3 oz) pitted black olives, drained

1 teaspoon dried oregano

200 g (7 oz) can tuna in olive oil, separated
   into large flakes and oil reserved

2 tablespoons dairy-free cream cheese

375 g (12 oz) dried tagliatelle pasta

pepper

handful of chopped flat-leaf parsley
   leaves, to garnish

1 Heat the garlic in the oil in a medium saucepan, then stir in the tomatoes, measurement water, ketchup, olives and oregano. Bring almost to the boil, then reduce the heat and simmer, part-covered, for 10 minutes until the sauce has reduced and thickened. Add the tuna with its oil, then stir in the cream cheese and cook briefly until heated through. Season with pepper.

2 Meanwhile, cook the pasta in a large saucepan of boiling water according to the packet instructions. Drain, reserving 4 tablespoons of the water, and return the pasta to the pan.

3 Toss the sauce with the pasta and reserved cooking water. Garnish with the chopped parsley and serve.

mac with no cheese

Serves 4

Preparation time 15 minutes

Cooking time 20 minutes

300 g (10 oz) dried macaroni or pasta shells

1 teaspoon vegetable bouillon powder

100 g (3½ oz) dairy-free strong Cheddar cheese alternative, grated

1¼ recipe quantities Dairy-free White Sauce (*see* page 138)

2 tomatoes, sliced

1 tablespoon olive oil

65 g (2½ oz) coarse fresh breadcrumbs

2 garlic cloves, finely chopped

steamed peas and carrots, to serve

This dairy-free version of a popular family meal is topped with a mouthwatering layer of crispy garlicky crumbs.

1 Cook the pasta in a large saucepan of boiling water according to the packet instructions. Drain, then tip the pasta into an ovenproof dish.

2 Stir the bouillon powder and cheese into the white sauce and heat through, stirring, until the cheese has melted into the sauce. Spoon the sauce over the pasta and mix until well combined. Place the slices of tomato on top and cook under a preheated medium-hot grill for a few minutes until the tomato has softened and is starting to colour.

3 Meanwhile, heat the oil in a large frying pan over a medium heat, add the breadcrumbs and fry for 3 minutes until golden and crisp. Reduce the heat slightly, add the garlic and cook for a further 1 minute, stirring to prevent the garlic burning.

4 Sprinkle the macaroni with the garlicky crumbs and serve with steamed peas and carrots.

sausage pasta bake

Serves 4

Preparation time 15 minutes

Cooking time 35–40 minutes

6 good-quality herby sausages

1 tablespoon olive oil

2 large garlic cloves, finely chopped

1½ x 400 g (13 oz) cans chopped tomatoes

1 tablespoon tomato purée

375 g (12 oz) dried penne pasta

3 tablespoons dairy-free garlic and herb cream cheese

100 g (3½ oz) dairy-free mozzarella cheese alternative, grated

This delicious pasta dish can be made in advance up to the end of step 4, then simply baked in the oven just before serving.

1 Squeeze the meat out of the sausage skins and shape into small balls – you'll get about 5 balls per sausage. Heat the oil in a large saucepan over a medium heat and cook the sausage balls for 5 minutes, turning occasionally, until browned all over. Remove the sausage balls with a slotted spoon and set aside.

2 Add the garlic, tomatoes and tomato purée to the pan, reduce the heat to medium-low and bring to the boil. Reduce the heat to low and simmer, part-covered, for 10 minutes, stirring frequently, until reduced and thickened.

3 Meanwhile, cook the pasta in a large saucepan of boiling water according to the packet instructions. Drain, reserving 4 tablespoons of the cooking water, and return the pasta and reserved cooking water to the pan.

4 Stir the sausage balls, tomato sauce and cream cheese into the pasta and warm through. Tip into a medium-sized ovenproof dish and scatter the mozzarella over the top.

5 Cover with a lid or foil and bake in a preheated oven, 190°C (375°F), Gas Mark 5, for 10 minutes, then remove the foil and cook for a further 10 minutes until starting to colour on top.

lamb, quinoa & mint patties

Serves 4

Preparation time 20 minutes

Cooking time 16 minutes

500 g (1 lb) minced lamb

2 teaspoons ground coriander

1 teaspoon ground cumin

1 teaspoon paprika

1 teaspoon dried mint

½ teaspoon dried chilli flakes (optional)

2 garlic cloves, crushed

100 g (3½ oz) cooked quinoa or bulgar wheat

olive oil, for frying and drizzling

salt and pepper

To serve

2 tomatoes, deseeded and diced

1 small red onion, sliced

handful of mint leaves, roughly chopped

1 recipe quantity Tahini Dip (*see* page 137) or dairy-free mayonnaise

4 flatbreads

1 Mix together the lamb, spices, mint, chilli flakes, if using, garlic and cooked grain in a large bowl and season. Using wet hands, shape the mixture into 12 patties, each about 5 cm (2 inches) across.

2 Heat a large griddle pan over a high heat, then reduce the heat slightly and brush one side of the patties with oil. Griddle half the patties, oil side down, for 4 minutes. Brush the tops of the patties with a little extra oil, then turn them over and cook for a further 4 minutes until golden and cooked through. Remove from the griddle and cover with foil. Keep warm in the bottom of a low oven while you cook the remaining patties.

3 Meanwhile, mix together the tomatoes, onion and mint in a serving bowl and drizzle with a little oil. Set aside. Put the tahini dip or mayonnaise in a separate serving bowl. Wrap the flatbreads in foil and warm through in the low oven.

4 Put the patties on a serving plate and let everyone help themselves to the flatbreads, patties and toppings.

tofu steaks with egg rice

Serves 4

**Preparation time 20 minutes,
plus marinating**

Cooking time 25 minutes

3 tablespoons hoisin sauce

1 tablespoon sesame oil, plus extra
to serve

1 tablespoon reduced-salt soy sauce,
plus extra to serve

400 g (13 oz) firm tofu, drained, patted
dry and cut into 8 slices

1 tablespoon sunflower oil or coconut
oil, plus extra for greasing

150 g (5 oz) frozen peas

6 spring onions, thinly sliced

1 red pepper, cored, deseeded and thinly
sliced

2.5 cm (1 inch) piece of fresh root ginger,
peeled and finely chopped

75 g (3 oz) white cabbage, finely shredded

2 garlic cloves, finely chopped

575 g (1¼ lb) cooked brown basmati rice

4 eggs

pepper

If you're using leftover rice to make this
dish, do make sure it is heated through really
thoroughly before serving. Alternatively,
cook about 200 g (7 oz) dried rice, then
refresh under cold running water.

1 Mix together the hoisin sauce, sesame oil and soy sauce in a
shallow dish. Add the tofu and spoon the marinade over until
coated. Leave to marinate for at least 30 minutes.

2 Lightly oil a large baking sheet. Turn the tofu in the marinade,
then arrange the slices in the baking sheet. Place in a preheated
oven, 190°C (375°F), Gas Mark 5, for 25 minutes, turning once,
or until golden and starting to crisp.

3 Meanwhile, cook the peas in a small saucepan of boiling water
for 3–4 minutes, then drain.

4 Heat the sunflower or coconut oil in a large wok or frying
pan, add 5 of the spring onions, the red pepper, ginger and
cabbage and stir-fry for 3 minutes until softened. Add the garlic
and rice and stir-fry for 3 minutes until the rice is piping hot.

5 Make a hole in the centre of the rice and crack in the eggs,
then cook for a minute or so until they start to set. Start to
fold the eggs into the rice so they cook in large flakes – about
2–3 minutes. Season with pepper, add a good splash of sesame
oil and soy sauce and stir in the peas. Turn the rice again and
serve sprinkled with the remaining spring onion and topped
with the tofu.

peanutty noodles

Serves 4

Preparation time 15 minutes

Cooking time 10 minutes

1 tablespoon sunflower oil or coconut oil

150 g (5 oz) mushrooms, sliced

2 garlic cloves

1 recipe quantity Satay Dip (*see* page 28)

200 g (7 oz) broccoli, cut into small florets

450 g (14½ oz) ready-cooked udon noodles

100 ml (3½ fl oz) water

2 spring onions, thinly sliced diagonally

3 tablespoons roasted unsalted peanuts, roughly chopped

Noodles always go down well with kids and this dish will hopefully become a family favourite. It uses thick udon noodles but you could use egg or wholewheat noodles instead.

1 Heat the oil in a large wok or frying pan, add the mushrooms and stir-fry for 7 minutes until soft and starting to crisp. Add the garlic and cook for a further 1 minute, then stir in the satay dip.

2 Meanwhile, steam the broccoli for 5 minutes until just tender, then refresh under cold running water.

3 Add the noodles to the satay mushrooms, separating them with your fingers, then reduce the heat to low and add the measurement water and broccoli. Heat through until piping hot, adding a splash more water if necessary.

4 Serve the noodles sprinkled with the spring onions and peanuts.

Tips and tricks

For a more substantial meal, you could also top the noodles with cubes of smoked tofu, slices of omelette or cooked prawns.

salmon & potato tortilla

Serves 3–4

Preparation time 15 minutes

Cooking time 30–40 minutes

3 tablespoons olive oil

3 potatoes, such as Maris Piper or King
Edwards, about 550 g (1 lb 3 oz) total
weight, peeled and cubed

1 large onion, sliced

100 g (3½ oz) frozen petits pois

200 g (7 oz) can red salmon, drained, skin
and bones removed and fish flaked

6 large eggs, lightly beaten

15 g (½ oz) dairy-free spread

salt and pepper

1 Heat the oil in a medium ovenproof frying pan over a medium heat. Reduce the heat, add the potatoes and cook for about 15–20 minutes, turning occasionally, until tender. Remove with a slotted spoon and transfer to a bowl.

2 Pour off all but 1 tablespoon of the oil, reduce the heat slightly and add the onion to the pan. Cook for 8 minutes, stirring occasionally, until softened.

3 Meanwhile, steam the peas until tender, then add to the bowl with the potatoes. Add the cooked onion, salmon and eggs to the bowl, season with salt and pepper and turn gently until combined.

4 Wipe out the frying pan, then melt the spread over a medium-low heat. Pour in the egg mixture in an even layer, making sure the potatoes, peas, onion and salmon are evenly distributed. Cook for 6–8 minutes until the base is light golden and set, then place under a preheated medium grill and cook for 2–3 minutes until the top is just set. Serve cut into wedges.

bbq mushroom burgers

Serves 4

Preparation time 15 minutes,
  plus marinating

Cooking time 20–25 minutes

4 tablespoons tomato ketchup

2 tablespoons reduced-salt soy sauce

1 tablespoon balsamic vinegar

1 tablespoon honey or maple syrup

1 tablespoon olive oil

4 large flat mushrooms, wiped and stalks
  removed

75 g (3 oz) silken tofu, drained and
  roughly chopped

To serve

3 tomatoes, deseeded and diced

2 spring onions, finely chopped

½ red pepper, cored, deseeded and diced

shredded crisp lettuce

4 soft seeded wholemeal buns, split open
  and lightly toasted

Barbecue sauce is simple to make and adds a lovely flavour and colour to these simple mushroom burgers.

1 Mix together the ketchup, soy sauce, vinegar, honey or maple syrup and oil in a bowl. Brush two-thirds of the barbecue sauce all over the mushrooms, then transfer the mushrooms to a roasting tin. Place in a preheated oven, 200° (400°F), Gas Mark 6, for 20–25 minutes or until tender.

2 Meanwhile, add the tofu to the remaining barbecue sauce and blend with a stick blender until smooth and thick.

3 Mix together the tomatoes, spring onions and red pepper in a bowl. Place some shredded lettuce on top of the toasted bun bases. Top each with a mushroom, then add a spoonful each of the creamy barbecue sauce and tomato relish. Top with the bun lids and serve.

sausage & broccoli tart

Serves 4

Preparation time 15 minutes

Cooking time 40 minutes

1 tablespoon olive oil, plus extra for greasing and brushing

1 onion, thinly sliced

1 large garlic clove, thinly sliced

125 ml (4 fl oz) passata

1 tablespoon tomato purée

1 teaspoon dried thyme

320 g (11 oz) dairy-free ready-rolled puff pastry

4 herby pork sausages

beaten egg, to glaze

200 g (7 oz) broccoli, cut into small florets

salt and pepper

Most shop-bought, ready-made puff pastry is dairy-free, but it always pays to check the packaging – you obviously want to avoid the 'all-butter' variety. This is a very simple tart to make and just needs the addition of new potatoes and vegetables.

1 Lightly grease a large baking sheet.

2 Heat the oil in a large frying pan over a medium-low heat, add the onion and cook for 10 minutes until softened, reducing the heat if the onion starts to brown. Stir in the garlic 1 minute before the end of the cooking time, then remove the pan from the heat.

3 Mix together the passata, tomato purée and thyme in a bowl, then season with salt and pepper.

4 Unroll the sheet of pastry and place it on the prepared baking sheet. Score a border about 1 cm (½ inch) in from the edge and roll the edges up slightly. Spread the tomato mixture over the pastry within the border. Spoon over the onion in an even layer.

5 Squeeze the meat out of the sausage skins in bite-sized balls and place evenly over the tart. Brush the balls with oil, then brush the edges of the pastry with egg. Place in a preheated oven, 200°C (400°F), Gas Mark 6, for 20 minutes.

6 Meanwhile, steam the broccoli florets until just tender. Arrange the broccoli on top of the tart, brush with a little oil and return to the oven for a further 10 minutes or until the pastry is cooked and golden.

chorizo & bean hotpot with sweet potato mash

Serves 4

Preparation time 15 minutes

Cooking time 25 minutes

1 tablespoon olive oil

1 large onion, chopped

250 g (8 oz) chorizo sausage, skin removed and cut into bite-sized chunks

2 garlic cloves, chopped

1 teaspoon dried oregano

400 g (13 oz) can chopped tomatoes

1 tablespoon tomato purée

1 teaspoon smoked paprika

400 g (13 oz) can baked beans

salt and pepper

chopped fresh coriander, to garnish

Sweet potato mash

625 g (1 lb 6 oz) sweet potatoes, peeled and cut into large chunks

1 large garlic clove, sliced

2–3 tablespoons dairy-free mayonnaise

This hotpot has a real Spanish feel, despite the addition of baked beans!

1 Heat the oil in a large heavy-based saucepan over a medium heat, add the onion and cook for 6 minutes, stirring frequently, until softened. Stir in the chorizo and cook for a further 3 minutes. Add the garlic and continue to cook for 1 minute.

2 Add the oregano, tomatoes, tomato purée and smoked paprika. Fill the empty tomato can one-third full with water, swill it around and add the liquid to the pan. Bring to the boil, then reduce the heat and simmer, part-covered, for 10 minutes until the sauce has reduced and thickened. Stir in the beans, season with salt and pepper and heat through.

3 Meanwhile, make the mash. Cook the sweet potatoes and garlic in a saucepan of boiling water for 12–15 minutes until tender, then drain and return the potatoes to the pan to dry. Add the mayonnaise and mash until smooth.

4 Serve the hotpot, sprinkled with coriander, with the mash.

Tips and tricks

You could, of course, replace the beans with a can of chickpeas or another favourite pulse and increase the quantity of canned tomatoes by 200 g (7 oz).

omelette 'pizzas'

Serves 2

Preparation time 10 minutes

Cooking time 10 minutes

20 g (¾ oz) dairy-free spread

4 eggs

½ small red onion, thinly sliced into rings

1 tomato, deseeded and diced

2 mushrooms, thinly sliced

handful of pitted olives, halved

2 teaspoons dairy-free pesto, or
   homemade Tomato Pesto (*see* page 53)

2 tablespoons dairy-free cream cheese or
   grated mozzarella cheese alternative

extra virgin olive oil, for drizzling

1 Heat half the spread in a medium-sized ovenproof frying pan over a medium heat. Lightly beat 2 of the eggs in a bowl, then pour into the pan. Turn the pan until the eggs coat the base in an even layer, then cook until the bottom of the omelette is set but the top is still slightly runny.

2 Arrange half the onion, tomato, mushrooms and olives over the top. Dot half the pesto and cheese on top, then drizzle with a little oil. Place under a preheated medium grill and cook for 2 minutes or until just cooked. Keep warm in a low oven.

3 Repeat with the remaining ingredients to make a second 'pizza'. Slip on to a serving plate and serve hot.

weekends

summer rolls

Makes 12

Preparation time 20 minutes

Cooking time 3 minutes

50 g (2 oz) vermicelli rice noodles

1 teaspoon sesame oil

12 rice paper wrappers

7 cm (3 inch) piece of cucumber, deseeded and cut into long, thin strips

½ red pepper, cored, deseeded and cut into long, thin strips

2 spring onions, halved and cut into long, thin strips

175 g (6 oz) large cooked peeled prawns, sliced in half lengthways

1 tablespoon sesame seeds, toasted

handful of basil leaves

Dipping sauce

2 tablespoons hoisin sauce, plus extra for drizzling

1 tablespoon reduced-salt soy sauce

juice of 1 lime

honey, to taste

Get the kids to help you make these rice paper rolls, which are filled with prawns and fresh vegetables – have all the fillings prepared before you soak the wrappers. They are lots of fun to make and can be served as a lunch or with a stir-fry for a more filling meal.

1 Cook the rice noodles according to the packet instructions, then drain and toss in the sesame oil.

2 Meanwhile, mix together all the dipping sauce ingredients in a bowl.

3 To assemble the rolls, pour hot water into a large bowl. Place a rice paper wrapper flat in the water until pliable, but not too soft. Carefully remove the wrapper from the bowl using a spatula and place flat on a chopping board.

4 Drizzle a little hoisin sauce horizontally near the bottom of the wrapper and top with a few strips of cucumber, red pepper and spring onion, 3 halves of prawns, a sprinkling of sesame seeds and a couple of basil leaves. (Be careful not to overfill as this makes the wrapper difficult to fold.)

5 Bring the bottom edge of the wrapper tightly over the filling and tuck in the sides, then continue to roll up to encase the filling. Put the rice paper roll on a plate, seam side down. Repeat with the remaining ingredients to make 12 rolls.

6 Serve the summer rolls with the dipping sauce.

beef & lentil lasagne

Serves 4–6

Preparation time 20 minutes

Cooking time 1 hour 35 minutes

2 tablespoons olive oil

1 large onion, chopped

1 carrot, diced

1 celery stick, diced

2 large garlic cloves, chopped

200 g (7 oz) streaky bacon, roughly chopped

400 g (13 oz) lean minced beef

200 ml (7 fl oz) red wine or extra stock

400 g (13 oz) can chopped tomatoes

2 tablespoons tomato purée

250 ml (8 fl oz) beef stock

2 tablespoons each chopped sage, parsley and thyme

2 bay leaves

400 g (13 oz) can green lentils, rinsed and drained

12 fresh lasagne sheets

1 recipe quantity Dairy-free White Sauce (*see* page 138)

2 tablespoons crispy fried onions (optional)

salt and pepper

We all know that we should be cutting back on the amount of meat we eat. Consequently, this delicious lasagne goes easy on the beef, but includes canned lentils to give it extra substance.

1 Heat half the oil in a large heavy-based saucepan over a medium heat, add the onion and cook for 5 minutes until softened. Add the carrot and celery and cook for a further 5 minutes, then stir in the garlic. Remove the vegetables from the pan and set aside.

2 Add the remaining oil to the pan and cook the bacon for 5 minutes until golden. Remove from the pan with a slotted spoon, add the mince and cook for about 5 minutes until browned. Return the onion mixture and bacon to the pan and pour in the wine or extra stock. Let it bubble away for 5 minutes or until there is no aroma of alcohol.

3 Add the tomatoes, tomato purée, stock and herbs to the pan and bring to the boil, then reduce the heat and simmer, part-covered, for 25 minutes, stirring occasionally. Add the lentils, season with salt and pepper and cook for a further 5 minutes until heated through – remove the lid if the sauce is too thin.

4 To assemble the lasagne, spoon one-third of the meat sauce into a 1.8 litre (3 pint) ovenproof dish. Top with a layer of lasagne, then spread over one-third of the white sauce. Repeat with another 2 layers of meat sauce, lasagne and white sauce. Sprinkle the crispy onions over the top, if using.

5 Cook in a preheated oven, 180°C (350°F), Gas Mark 4, for 35–40 minutes until the lasagne is cooked through.

bacon & pea flan

Serves 4

Preparation time 20 minutes

Cooking time 1 hour 5 minutes

20 g (¾ oz) dairy-free spread, plus extra for greasing

325 g (11 oz) dairy-free shortcrust pastry

flour, for dusting

8 smoked bacon rashers

2 large onions, finely chopped

75 g (3 oz) frozen petits pois

2 large eggs

200 ml (7 fl oz) unsweetened almond milk (*see* page 134 for homemade) or other dairy-free milk

100 ml (3½ fl oz) dairy-free cream

1 teaspoon Dijon mustard

1 tablespoon nutritional yeast flakes

1 teaspoon dried thyme

salt and pepper

Nutritional yeast flakes can be bought in health food shops or online and make a nutritious alternative to cheese, thanks to their cheesy flavour. They are especially good in sauces as they dissolve when heated.

1 Lightly grease a 23 cm (9 inch) loose-bottomed flan tin.

2 Roll out the pastry on a lightly floured work surface and use to line the prepared flan tin. Line the pastry case with baking paper and baking beans, then bake in a preheated oven, 180°C (350°F), Gas Mark 4, for 15 minutes. Remove the beans and paper and return the case to the oven for a further 15 minutes until the pastry is crisp and light golden.

3 Meanwhile, put the bacon on a foil-lined baking sheet and place it in the oven to cook alongside the pastry case for 15–20 minutes, turning once, until golden and starting to crisp. Drain the bacon on kitchen paper to remove any excess fat.

4 While the pastry case and bacon are cooking, heat the spread in a large frying pan over a medium-low heat and gently cook the onions for 20 minutes until very soft, reducing the heat if they start to colour. Steam the peas in a separate saucepan until tender.

5 Whisk together the eggs, milk, cream, mustard, yeast flakes and thyme in a jug, then season with salt and pepper.

6 Spoon the onions and peas over the pastry case in an even layer. Cut the bacon into bite-sized pieces and scatter over the top. Pour the egg mixture into the pastry case and bake for 35 minutes or until just set and starting to colour.

smoked salmon & kale risotto

Serves 4

Preparation time 15 minutes

Cooking time 40 minutes

15 g (½ oz) dairy-free spread

1 tablespoon olive oil

1 large onion, finely chopped

350 g (11½ oz) risotto rice

175 ml (6 fl oz) dry white wine or
  extra stock

1.2 litres (2 pints) hot fish stock

75 g (3 oz) kale, tough stalks discarded
  and leaves finely chopped, or small
  broccoli florets

1 heaped tablespoon dairy-free
  cream cheese

150 g (5 oz) smoked salmon pieces

handful of chives, snipped

juice of ½ lemon

pepper

1 Heat the spread and oil in a large heavy-based saucepan over a medium-low heat, add the onion and cook gently for 10 minutes, stirring frequently, until softened but not coloured. Add the rice and stir to coat it in the onion mixture.

2 Pour the wine or extra stock into the pan and let it bubble away, stirring, for 5 minutes until absorbed by the rice and there is no aroma of alcohol. Start to add the stock, a ladleful at a time, stirring continuously. Only add the next ladleful of stock when the previous one has been absorbed, and continue until the rice is creamy with just a slight bite – about 25 minutes. The risotto should be slightly soupy and not dry.

3 Meanwhile, steam the kale or broccoli until tender, then refresh under cold running water.

4 When the rice is cooked, remove the pan from the heat, season with pepper and stir in the kale, cream cheese, smoked salmon, half the chives and the lemon juice. Stir gently but thoroughly until combined. Cover and leave to stand on the warm hob for a couple of minutes to heat through. Serve sprinkled with the remaining chives.

Tips and tricks

Although there is wine in this creamy salmon risotto for added flavour, the alcohol is actually burnt off so there is no trace left, but you can use extra stock instead of the wine, if preferred.

pea & mint risotto

Serves 4

Preparation time 20 minutes

Cooking time 40 minutes

2 tablespoons olive oil

2 leeks, trimmed, cleaned and finely chopped

350 g (11½ oz) risotto rice

175 ml (6 fl oz) dry white wine or extra stock

1.5 litres (2½ pints) hot vegetable stock

300 g (10 oz) frozen peas

handful of mint leaves, chopped

handful of basil leaves

4 tablespoons nutritional yeast flakes

4 eggs

salt and pepper

1 Heat the oil in a large heavy-based saucepan, add the leeks, cover and sauté for 5 minutes, stirring occasionally, until very soft and tender. Add the rice and stir for a couple of minutes to coat it in the leek mixture.

2 Pour the wine into the pan and let it bubble away, stirring, for 5 minutes until absorbed by the rice and there is no aroma of alcohol. Start to add the stock, a ladleful at a time, stirring continuously. Only add the next ladleful of stock when the previous one has been absorbed by the rice and continue until the rice is creamy with just a slight bite – about 25 minutes. The rice should be slightly soupy and not dry.

3 Meanwhile, steam the peas until tender. Tip them into a blender or food processor, add the mint, basil and 100 ml (3½ fl oz) of the stock and blend until puréed, then set aside.

4 When the risotto is cooked, turn off the heat and stir in the pea purée and three-quarters of the yeast flakes. Season to taste, cover and leave to stand on the warm hob until ready to serve.

5 Meanwhile, bring a large sauté pan of water to the boil, then reduce the heat to a simmer. Break an egg into a cup. Swirl the water and slip the egg into the pan, then repeat with the remaining 3 eggs. Simmer, occasionally spooning the water over the top of the eggs, until the whites are set but the yolks remain runny.

6 Top each serving of the risotto with a poached egg and serve sprinkled with the remaining yeast flakes.

thai tofu burgers

Serves 4

Preparation time 20 minutes, plus chilling

Cooking time 16 minutes

500 g (1 lb) firm tofu, drained, patted dry
and coarsely grated

4 teaspoons Thai red curry paste

3 garlic cloves, finely chopped

2.5 cm (1 inch) piece of fresh root ginger,
peeled and grated

4 spring onions, finely chopped

1½ tablespoons reduced-salt soy sauce

1 large egg white

3 tablespoons plain flour

sunflower oil, for frying

pepper

Sweet chilli dip

3 tablespoons dairy-free mayonnaise

2 tablespoons sweet chilli sauce

juice of ½ lime

To serve

4 mini naan breads, warmed

1 Little Gem lettuce, shredded

5 cm (2 inch) piece of cucumber, sliced

1 spring onion, thinly shredded

1 Place the tofu in a bowl and stir in the curry paste, garlic, ginger, spring onions, soy sauce, egg white and flour. Season with pepper and stir thoroughly until combined. Cover and chill for about 30 minutes to let the flavours meld.

2 Using wet hands, shape the tofu mixture into 8 small burgers. Heat enough oil to generously coat the base of a large frying pan. Fry the tofu burgers, in 2 batches, for 4 minutes on each side until golden and cooked through. Remove with a slotted spoon, drain on kitchen paper and keep warm in a low oven while you cook the remaining burgers.

3 Meanwhile, make the sweet chilli dip. Mix together the mayo, sweet chilli sauce and lime juice in a bowl until combined.

4 To serve, spoon the sweet chilli dip over the warm naan breads, then top with the shredded lettuce, tofu burgers, cucumber and spring onions.

Tips and tricks

Tofu makes surprisingly good, nutritious burgers, but because of its mild flavour you do need to be generous with the flavourings.

coconutty fish curry

Serves 4

Preparation time 15 minutes,
  plus marinating

Cooking time 30 minutes

2 tablespoons olive oil

1 large onion, coarsely grated

3 garlic cloves, coarsely grated

1½ teaspoons turmeric

200 g (7 oz) raw peeled king prawns

400 g (13 oz) thick skinless, boneless
  white fish fillets, cut into large bite-
  sized chunks

2.5 cm (1 inch) piece of fresh root ginger,
  peeled and finely chopped

1 large red pepper, cored, deseeded
  and chopped

400 ml (14 fl oz) can coconut milk

150 ml (¼ pint) fish stock

1–2 teaspoons mild chilli powder, to taste
  (optional)

3 tablespoons tomato purée

2 large handfuls of coriander leaves,
  chopped

salt and pepper

To serve

Thai sticky rice

lime wedges

I would recommend trying this mild, creamy coconut fish curry as a great way to encourage kids to eat both seafood and spices. Serve it with steamed rice and vegetables.

1 Mix together half the oil, one-third of the onion and garlic and half the turmeric in a large bowl. Season with salt and pepper, then add the prawns and fish and turn gently to coat them in the marinade. Cover and leave to marinate in the refrigerator for at least 30 minutes.

2 Heat the remaining oil in a medium saucepan over a medium-low heat, add the remaining onion and cook for 8 minutes, stirring frequently, until softened. Reduce the heat to low, add the remaining garlic, the ginger and red pepper and cook for 3 minutes, stirring frequently.

3 Pour in the coconut milk and stock and bring to the boil, then reduce the heat, stir in the chilli powder, if using, tomato purée and the remaining turmeric and simmer for 15 minutes, stirring occasionally, until reduced by one-third.

4 Add half the coriander, the prawns, fish and marinade and cook for 3 minutes or until the prawns have turned pink and the fish is cooked through, then season to taste.

5 Sprinkle with the remaining coriander and serve with rice and lime wedges for squeezing over.

salmon & leek pie

Serves 4

Preparation time 20 minutes

Cooking time 50 minutes

875 g (1¾ lb) potatoes, peeled and quartered

40 g (1½ oz) dairy-free spread

1 tablespoon olive oil

2 large leeks, trimmed, cleaned and thinly sliced

125 g (4 oz) frozen peas

2 tablespoons plain flour

1 large garlic clove, finely chopped

150 g (5 oz) dairy-free cream cheese

2 tablespoons lemon juice

2 heaped teaspoons English mustard

handful of parsley, finely chopped

275 ml (9 fl oz) unsweetened dairy-free milk

500 g (1 lb) skinless salmon fillets, cut into large bite-sized pieces

75 g (3 oz) smoked salmon pieces

salt and pepper

This makes a great alternative Sunday lunch to the usual roast dinner. The pie uses just salmon but you could use a combination of fish, including perhaps a smoked one.

1 Cook the potatoes in a large saucepan of salted boiling water for 10–15 minutes until tender, then drain and return to the pan.

2 Meanwhile, heat half the spread and the oil in a large frying pan over a medium-low heat, add the leeks, cover and sauté for 10 minutes until very soft but not coloured.

3 Steam the peas in a separate pan, then drain and set aside.

4 Stir the flour into the leeks and continue to cook over a low heat for 2 minutes, stirring continuously. Turn off the heat but leave the pan on the warm hob and stir in the garlic, cream cheese, lemon juice, mustard, parsley and 200 ml (7 fl oz) of the milk until combined. Fold in the salmon, smoked salmon and peas and season to taste.

5 Add the remaining spread and 50 ml (2 fl oz) of the milk to the potatoes. Warm briefly, then mash until smooth, adding the remaining milk if necessary. Season to taste.

6 Spoon the salmon mixture into a 1.8 litre (3 pint) ovenproof dish. Top with the mashed potato and run a fork over the top to give a slightly rough texture. Bake in a preheated oven, 200°C (400°F), Gas Mark 6, for 30 minutes or until the salmon is cooked through and the top is golden and crisp.

piri piri chicken

Serves 4

**Preparation time 15 minutes,
 plus marinating**

Cooking time 30–40 minutes

6–8 chicken thighs, depending on
 their size, bone in and skin on

1 large red pepper, cored, deseeded
 and sliced

1 mild red chilli, deseeded and
 quartered (optional)

1 garlic clove, halved

1 tablespoon red wine vinegar

1 teaspoon paprika

1 tablespoon chopped flat leaf
 parsley leaves

salt and pepper

To serve (optional)
roast potato wedges
mixed salad

Serve the chicken with baked potato wedges, which can be put in the oven at the same time as the thighs, or rice and a salad. If you want to avoid the chilli in this zingy red pepper marinade, then you can leave it out without detrimentally affecting the flavour.

1 Make 3 diagonal cuts in the skin of each chicken thigh, then transfer to a large, shallow non-reactive dish.

2 Blend together the remaining ingredients in a food processor or blender until smooth, then spoon over the chicken thighs and turn until well coated. Cover and leave to marinate in the refrigerator for at least 30 minutes.

3 Transfer the chicken thighs to a roasting tin and spoon over any sauce left in the dish. Roast in a preheated oven, 190°C (375°F), Gas Mark 5, for 30–40 minutes or until cooked through and golden.

4 Serve with roast potato wedges and a mixed salad, if liked.

oven-baked falafel

Serves 3–4

Preparation time 15 minutes, plus chilling

Cooking time 20–30 minutes

400 g (13 oz) can chickpeas, rinsed and drained

1 small onion, quartered

2 garlic cloves, halved

1 heaped teaspoon ground cumin

2 heaped teaspoons ground coriander

1 teaspoon dried mint

½ teaspoon harissa paste (optional)

1 tablespoon extra virgin olive oil, plus extra for greasing and brushing

2 tablespoons gram flour

salt and pepper

To serve

4 pitta breads, warmed

4 tablespoons hummus

few drops of chilli sauce (optional)

shredded Little Gem lettuce

2 tomatoes, sliced

few slices of cucumber

salad leaves

potato wedges

This makes a great Saturday-night-in-front-of-the-TV type of meal, where everyone can help themselves to the falafel, warm pitta bread and other fillings. It is much easier to bake the falafel in the oven as they can all be cooked in one go, rather than fried in batches, and this also keeps the fat level down.

1 Put the chickpeas, onion, garlic, spices, mint, harissa, if using, and oil in a food processor or blender and whizz to a coarse paste. Stir in the gram flour and season. Shape the mixture into 12 patties, each about the size of a flattened golf ball. Cover and chill for 30 minutes to firm up.

2 Lightly grease a large baking sheet. Brush both sides of the falafel with oil and transfer to the sheet. Place in a preheated oven, 190°C (375°F), Gas Mark 5, and cook for 20–30 minutes, turning once, until golden and crisp.

3 Split the warmed pitta breads open and spread with the hummus, adding a splash of chilli sauce, if liked. Fill each pitta with lettuce, falafel, tomatoes and cucumber. Serve with salad and potato wedges.

sweet & sour pork balls

Serves 4

Preparation time 25 minutes

Cooking time 15 minutes

2 large garlic cloves, finely chopped

2.5 cm (1 inch) piece of unpeeled fresh root ginger, grated

500 g (1 lb) minced pork

2 spring onions, finely chopped

2 tablespoons reduced-salt soy sauce

½ teaspoon Chinese 5-spice powder

1 tablespoon sesame oil

1 tablespoon cornflour

1 egg, lightly beaten

sunflower oil, for frying

300 g (10 oz) wholewheat noodles

salt and pepper

Sweet and sour sauce

2 large garlic cloves, finely chopped

2.5 cm (1 inch) piece of unpeeled fresh root ginger, grated

1 small red pepper, cored, deseeded and sliced

2 tomatoes, roughly chopped

2 tablespoons tomato ketchup

2 tablespoons reduced-salt soy sauce

1 tablespoon tomato purée

1 teaspoon honey

4 tablespoons water

1 To make the pork balls, put all the ingredients, except the sunflower oil, noodles and sauce ingredients in a bowl. Season with salt and pepper and stir until well combined. Using wet hands, shape the mixture into 20 walnut-sized balls. Cover and leave in the refrigerator to firm up while you prepare the sauce.

2 Place all the sauce ingredients in a food processor or blender and blend to a purée. Set aside.

3 Heat enough oil to generously cover the base of a large frying pan over a medium heat. Cook the pork balls, in 2 batches, for 6 minutes until browned all over and cooked through. Return all the pork balls to the pan, pour in the sweet and sour sauce and cook for a further 2–3 minutes until heated through, adding a splash of water if necessary.

4 Meanwhile, cook the noodles according to the packet instructions, then drain and divide among 4 bowls. Spoon over the pork balls and sauce and serve immediately.

pizza bombas

Makes 20

**Preparation time 40 minutes,
 plus proving**

Cooking time 25 minutes

5 g (¼ oz) instant dried yeast

2 teaspoons caster sugar

2 tablespoons extra virgin olive oil,
 plus extra for oiling

325 ml (11 fl oz) lukewarm water

500 g (1 lb) strong bread flour, plus extra
 for dusting

1½ teaspoons salt

Filling

20 g (¾ oz) dairy-free spread

250 g (8 oz) chestnut mushrooms, diced

2 large garlic cloves, finely chopped

1 teaspoon dried oregano

12 medium-thick slices of chorizo,
 roughly chopped

2 tablespoons dairy-free cream cheese

Tomato sauce

2 tablespoons extra virgin olive oil

1 large garlic clove, finely chopped

400 ml (14 fl oz) passata

1 tablespoon tomato purée

½ teaspoon caster sugar

1 teaspoon dried oregano

1 Stir together the yeast, sugar, olive oil and measurement water in a jug and leave to stand for 5 minutes. Sift the flour and salt into a large bowl and make a large well in the centre. Pour the yeast mixture into the well, then gradually draw the flour mixture into the liquid using a fork. Using your hands, combine to form a ball. Tip the dough out on a floured work surface and knead for 10 minutes until smooth and elastic. Place in a lightly oiled bowl, cover with clingfilm and leave to rise in a warm place for about 1½ hours until doubled in size.

2 Meanwhile, make the filling. Heat the spread in a large frying pan over a medium heat, add the mushrooms and cook for 10 minutes until any liquid in the pan has evaporated and the mushrooms start to crisp. Remove from the heat and stir in the garlic, oregano, chorizo and cream cheese. Set aside.

3 Make the tomato sauce. Heat the oil in a saucepan and add all the remaining ingredients. Stir and bring almost to the boil, then reduce the heat and simmer, part-covered, for 10 minutes until reduced and thickened.

4 Divide the dough into 20 equal-sized pieces, each about the size of a golf ball. Form a piece of dough into a flattish round and place a heaped teaspoon of the mushroom filling in the centre, then draw the sides of the dough up around the filling and press the edges together to seal into a ball. Lightly oil a large baking sheet and roll the ball in the oil until coated. Repeat with the remaining dough and filling, then leave to prove for 15 minutes.

5 Bake the bombas in a preheated oven, 200°C (400°F), Gas Mark 6, for 15 minutes until risen and golden. Reheat the tomato sauce and serve with the bombas.

beef & barbecue sauce kebabs

Serves 4

Preparation time 20 minutes,
 plus marinating

Cooking time 8 minutes

475 g (15 oz) lean beef fillet steak,
 cut into 32 large bite-sized cubes

24 cherry tomatoes

1 large red onion, halved and cut into
 16 wedges

Marinade

4 tablespoons tomato purée

2 tablespoons tomato ketchup

1 teaspoon Worcestershire sauce

1 tablespoon cider vinegar

2 teaspoons smoked paprika

1 tablespoon olive oil, plus extra
 for brushing

To serve

rice, bulgar wheat or couscous

1 recipe quantity Dairy-free Tzatziki
 (*see* page 136)

The barbecue sauce marinade gives these beef and vegetable kebabs a lovely smoky flavour and glossy coating. The kebabs are grilled but would also taste great barbecued.

1 Mix together all the marinade ingredients in a large, shallow non-reactive dish. Add the beef and turn until coated, then cover and leave to marinate in the refrigerator for at least 1 hour.

2 Starting and ending with the beef, thread the beef, cherry tomatoes and onion wedges on to 8 metal skewers. Turn the skewers in the marinade and brush with extra oil.

3 Arrange the skewers on a grill rack over a foil-lined grill pan. Cook under a preheated medium-high grill for 8 minutes until the vegetables are tender and the meat is just cooked through but not pink, turning occasionally and basting with more of the marinade to prevent the beef drying out.

4 Serve the kebabs with rice, bulgar wheat or couscous and spoonfuls of tzatziki.

creamy chicken & leek pie

Serves 4–6

Preparation time 20 minutes

Cooking time 1¼ hours

4 streaky bacon rashers

2 tablespoons olive oil

550 g (1 lb 3 oz) boneless, skinless chicken thighs, cut into large bite-sized chunks

1 large leek, trimmed, cleaned and chopped

250 g (8 oz) chestnut mushrooms, quartered

2 large garlic cloves, finely chopped

1½ teaspoons dried thyme

275 ml (9 fl oz) chicken stock

1 tablespoon cornflour

1 tablespoon water

2 tablespoons dairy-free cream cheese

400 g (13 oz) dairy-free puff pastry

flour, for dusting

a little dairy-free milk, to glaze

salt and pepper

1 Cook the bacon under a preheated hot grill until almost crisp, then drain on kitchen paper.

2 Meanwhile, heat half the oil in a large heavy-based pan over a medium-high heat, add half the chicken and cook for 5 minutes until browned all over, then remove from the pan with a slotted spoon and set aside. Repeat with the remaining chicken, adding a little of the remaining oil if necessary, then remove from the pan.

3 Heat the remaining oil in the pan, add the leek and cook for 5 minutes until softened. Add the mushrooms and cook for a further 5 minutes until tender, then stir in the browned chicken, the garlic and thyme. Pour in the stock and bring to the boil, then reduce the heat and simmer, part-covered, for 20 minutes until reduced.

4 Stir the cornflour into the measurement water in a cup, then add to the pan and cook for 5 minutes until the sauce has thickened, stirring frequently. Turn off the heat and stir in the cream cheese. Cut the bacon into pieces and add these to the pan, then season to taste.

5 Spoon the chicken filling into a 30 x 25 cm (12 x 10 inch) pie dish. Roll out the pastry on a lightly floured work surface so it is 7 cm (3 inches) larger than the top of the pie dish. Cut a 1.5 cm-(¾ inch-) wide strip of pastry the same length as the rim of the pie dish. Brush the rim of the pie dish with water, then place the pastry strip on top. Brush the pastry strip with a little water, then place the large sheet of pastry on top. Trim and crimp the edges, then decorate the top with any surplus pastry. Brush the top with milk and prick a few times with a fork.

6 Bake in a preheated oven, 220°C (425°F), Gas Mark 7, for 30 minutes until the pastry is golden and cooked.

pork hotpot with herby dumplings

Serves 4

Preparation time 25 minutes

Cooking time 1¾ hours

2 tablespoons olive oil

750 g (1 lb 10 oz) pork shoulder or leg, cut into large bite-sized pieces

2 onions, sliced

2 carrots, sliced

250 ml (8 fl oz) dry cider or extra stock

450 ml (¾ pint) chicken stock

2 bay leaves

2 teaspoons finely chopped rosemary

salt and pepper

Herby dumplings

100 g (3½ oz) self-raising flour, plus extra for dusting

⅓ teaspoon bicarbonate of soda

1 teaspoon dried thyme

1 teaspoon English mustard

100 ml (3½ fl oz) dairy-free yogurt, preferably unsweetened

The dumplings are light and fluffy and add the finishing touch to this warming, comforting, wintry meal.

1 Heat half the oil in a large heavy-based flameproof casserole over a medium heat, add the pork, in 2 batches, and cook for 5 minutes until browned all over. Remove the pork from the casserole and set aside.

2 Heat the remaining oil in the casserole, add the onions and cook for 5 minutes until softened, then stir in the carrots and cook for a further 2 minutes.

3 Pour in the cider or extra stock and let it bubble away until reduced by half and there is no aroma of alcohol. Pour in the stock, add the pork, bay leaves and rosemary and bring to the boil. Stir, then cover and transfer to a preheated oven, 170°C (340°F), Gas Mark 3½, for 1 hour.

4 Meanwhile, make the herby dumplings. Mix together the flour, bicarbonate of soda and thyme in a bowl. Stir in the mustard and yogurt, then using your hands, combine to form a ball. Divide the dough into 8 equal-sized pieces and, using floured hands, shape into dumplings. Arrange the dumplings in the casserole so they are half submerged. Re-cover and return to the oven for a further 15 minutes, then remove the lid and continue to cook for 10 minutes until they are light and fluffy.

picnic rolls

Makes 4

**Preparation time 20 minutes,
 plus standing**

4 crusty rolls

extra virgin olive oil, for brushing

6 tablespoons dairy-free pesto, or
 homemade Tomato Pesto (*see* page 53)

2 handfuls of baby spinach leaves

8 slices of roasted red pepper from a jar,
 drained

4 tablespoons dairy-free cream cheese

4 thick slices of ham

The filling is hidden inside these little rolls,
making them sturdy enough to transport.

1 Slice the top off each roll to form a lid and set aside. Pull out
the soft bread inside the bases and set aside, leaving a 1 cm
(½ inch) shell. Lightly brush the inside of each roll with oil.

2 Put the soft bread in a food processor and pulse to form
breadcrumbs. Mix half of the crumbs with the pesto.

3 Place a layer of spinach in the bottom of each roll and top
with a layer of pesto crumbs and all the red pepper. Spread with
the cream cheese and top with the ham, remaining crumbs
and spinach. Place the lids on top and wrap tightly in clingfilm.
Press down lightly and leave to stand for 30 minutes.

carrot & cabbage slaw

Serves 4

Preparation time 15 minutes

100 g (3½ oz) red cabbage, shredded

2 carrots, grated

3 spring onions, finely chopped

100 ml (3½ fl oz) dairy-free yogurt,
 preferably unsweetened

1 teaspoon wholegrain mustard

juice of 1 small lemon

pepper

This crisp and vibrant dairy-free version is a
real improvement on the usual ready-made
coleslaw sold in shops.

1 Mix together the cabbage, carrots, spring onions, yogurt,
mustard and lemon juice in a serving bowl. Season the slaw
with pepper to taste.

mini cheese & chive tarts

Makes 6

Preparation time 20 minutes, plus chilling

Cooking time 25–30 minutes

dairy-free spread, for greasing

320 g (11 oz) dairy-free ready-rolled
  puff pastry

flour, for dusting

150 ml (¼ pint) unsweetened
  dairy-free milk

3 tablespoons dairy-free cream

3 eggs

1 heaped teaspoon Dijon mustard

3 tablespoons nutritional yeast flakes

2 tablespoons snipped chives

3 cherry tomatoes, halved

These individual tarts are cooked in a jumbo muffin tray, which makes them much easier to make and also means they look really cute.

1 Lightly grease the holes of a 6-hole jumbo muffin tray. Roll out the pastry on a lightly floured work surface and use to line the prepared muffin holes, leaving the pastry slightly proud at the tops. Chill the pastry cases for 15 minutes.

2 Whisk together the milk, cream, eggs and mustard in a jug until combined, then stir in the yeast flakes and chives. Pour the mixture into the prepared pastry cases.

3 Place in a preheated oven, 200°C (400°F), Gas Mark 6, for 6–8 minutes until starting to set, then remove from the oven and place half a tomato on top of each tart. Return to the oven and continue to cook for another 19–22 minutes until risen and the pastry is cooked through. Leave to cool in the tin for 5 minutes, then turn out on to a wire rack. Serve warm or cold.

Indian lamb koftas

Serves 4

Preparation time 20 minutes, plus chilling

Cooking time 40 minutes

2 tablespoons sunflower oil

½ large onion, finely chopped

2 large garlic cloves, finely chopped

2.5 cm (1 inch) piece of fresh root ginger, peeled and finely chopped

400 g (13 oz) can chopped tomatoes

350 ml (12 fl oz) lamb stock

1 tablespoon tomato purée

2 teaspoons garam masala

1 teaspoon ground coriander

Koftas

½ large onion, cut into wedges

1 large garlic clove, peeled

2.5 cm (1 inch) piece of fresh root ginger, peeled

2 teaspoons garam masala

40 g (1½ oz) fresh breadcrumbs

300 g (10 oz) minced lamb

1 tablespoon tomato purée

salt and pepper

To serve

cooked brown basmati rice

4 tablespoons dairy-free yogurt, preferably unsweetened

handful of fresh coriander, chopped

1 red chilli, deseeded and finely chopped (optional)

These lightly spiced lamb meatballs are cooked in a mild curry sauce. If your children like slightly hot food, you could add a few chilli flakes to spice it up a little more.

1 Make the koftas. Put the onion, garlic and ginger in a food processor or blender and whizz to a coarse paste. Add the garam masala, breadcrumbs, lamb and tomato purée, season with salt and pepper and process briefly until combined. Shape the lamb mixture into 20 small walnut-sized balls, cover and chill for about 30 minutes.

2 Heat half the oil in a large saucepan, add the lamb koftas, in 2 batches, and cook for 5 minutes until golden all over. Remove from the pan and set aside.

3 Heat the remaining oil in the pan, add the onion and cook for 5 minutes until softened, then add the garlic and ginger and cook for a further 1 minute. Add the tomatoes, stock and tomato purée and bring to the boil. Reduce the heat and simmer for 5 minutes. Using a stick blender, purée the sauce until smooth, then stir in the garam masala and ground coriander.

4 Return the browned lamb koftas to the pan and simmer, part-covered, for 20 minutes, stirring occasionally, until the sauce has reduced and thickened.

5 Serve the koftas with rice, topped with yogurt, coriander and chilli, if liked.

tandoori roast chicken

Serves 4

Preparation time 15 minutes,
 plus marinating and resting

Cooking time 1 hour 20 minutes

1.5 kg (3 lb) chicken

250 ml (8 fl oz) water

1 recipe quantity Dairy-free Raita
 (*see* page 136), to serve

Tandoori marinade

3 tablespoons tandoori spice mix

2 teaspoons turmeric

3 garlic cloves, crushed

2.5 cm (1 inch) piece of unpeeled
 fresh root ginger, grated

juice of 1 lime

150 ml (¼ pint) dairy-free yogurt,
 preferably unsweetened

salt and pepper

A combination of dairy-free yogurt and spices makes a fantastic marinade for chicken and keeps it lovely and moist while roasting. The chicken is just as good served warm with roasties as it is cold with a salad and garlic mayonnaise.

1 Mix together all the marinade ingredients in a non-reactive bowl and season. Put the chicken on a plate and spoon the marinade over. Wearing a pair of rubber gloves, rub the marinade into the chicken until it is thoroughly coated all over. Cover the chicken with a double layer of clingfilm and leave to marinate in the refrigerator for at least 3 hours, or preferably overnight.

2 Place the chicken on a rack above a roasting tin and pour the measurement water into the tin (this will help to keep the chicken moist and can be used as a base for a gravy). Roast in a preheated oven, 200°C (400°F), Gas Mark 6, for about 1 hour 20 minutes, basting occasionally, until cooked through and the juices run clear when the thickest part of the thigh is pierced with a skewer. Remove the chicken from the oven, cover with a double layer of foil and leave to rest for 20 minutes. Carve into slices and serve with the Dairy-free Raita.

puddings

vanilla coconut balls

Serves 4

Preparation time 10 minutes,
plus cooling and freezing

Cooking time 2 minutes

8 tablespoons unsweetened
desiccated coconut

4 scoops of dairy-free vanilla ice cream

400 g (13 oz) fresh pineapple, or a
combination of pineapple, peach or
mango, cut into bite-sized pieces

To decorate (optional)

maple syrup or honey

toasted flaked almonds

This simple dessert takes shop-bought
dairy-free vanilla ice cream to a new level.

1 Put the coconut in a large, dry frying pan and toast for
2 minutes, tossing the pan occasionally, until golden. Tip the
coconut on to a plate and leave to cool.

2 Take a scoop of ice cream and roll it in the toasted coconut
until evenly coated. Repeat with the remaining ice cream and
coconut. Place the ice cream balls in the freezer for 10 minutes
to firm up slightly.

3 Spoon the fruit into 4 tall glasses and place a ball of
coconut-coated ice cream on top. Drizzle each with maple
syrup or honey and sprinkle with a few flaked almonds, if liked.

maple caramel fro-yo

Serves 6

**Preparation time 10 minutes,
  plus freezing**

2 bananas, chopped

125 ml (4 fl oz) coconut drinking milk
  (*see* page 135 for homemade)

125 ml (4 fl oz) dairy-free coconut yogurt

2 teaspoons vanilla extract

2 tablespoons maple syrup or honey

½ recipe quantity Dairy-free Caramel
  Sauce (*see* page 141)

1 Put all the ingredients except the caramel sauce in a food processor or blender and blend together until smooth and creamy. Spoon into a freezer-proof container with a lid and freeze for 3 hours or until ice crystals start to form.

2 Remove from the freezer and beat well to break up the ice crystals, then gently stir in the caramel sauce to form a swirly pattern. Return to the freezer for about 3 hours until frozen.

3 Remove the fro-yo from the freezer to soften about 20 minutes before serving.

Tips and tricks

You only need half the recipe quantity of the caramel sauce to swirl into the frozen yogurt; the rest will keep in the refrigerator for up to 5 days. The sauce is delicious spooned over fruit or dairy-free ice cream or yogurt, or used in the Raspberry & Caramel Trifles (*see* page 128).

mango kulfi

Serves 4

**Preparation time 15 minutes,
  plus freezing**

Cooking time 5 minutes

olive oil, for greasing

400 ml (14 fl oz) unsweetened almond
  milk (*see* page 134 for homemade)
  or other dairy-free milk

2 slices of white bread, crusts removed,
  torn into bite-sized pieces

1 large ripe mango, halved, stoned
  and sliced

2 tablespoons honey

1 teaspoon vanilla extract

To decorate (optional)

freshly grated nutmeg

2 tablespoons shelled pistachio nuts,
  toasted and chopped

1 Lightly grease 4 x 150 ml (¼ pint) metal pudding basin moulds with oil. Pour the almond milk into a medium-sized saucepan and bring almost to the boil, then add the bread and stir until it starts to break down.

2 Pour the mixture into a food processor or blender, add the mango, honey and vanilla extract and blend until smooth and creamy. Pour the mixture into the prepared moulds and freeze for about 3 hours until firm.

3 Remove from the freezer to soften about 20 minutes before serving. Turn the kulfi upside down and pour a little hot water over the base of each mould to release the kulfi. Place on serving plates, then grate over a little nutmeg and scatter with toasted pistachios, if liked.

forest fruit fools

Serves 4

Preparation time 15 minutes

150 g (5 oz) frozen black forest fruit mix, defrosted

125 ml (4 fl oz) dairy-free yogurt

4 tablespoons dairy-free soft cheese

1 large egg white

1 tablespoon caster sugar

handful of mixed berries, to decorate

Frozen fruit is a godsend and it's always useful to have a bag or two in the freezer to make fools, ice creams and smoothies or serve simply with dairy-free cream or custard.

1 Place the fruit, yogurt and soft cheese in a food processor or blender and blend together.

2 Whisk the egg white in a large, grease-free bowl until it holds its shape. Gradually add the sugar, whisking well between each addition, until the mixture is stiff and glossy, then fold into the fruit mixture using a metal spoon.

3 Spoon the fool into 4 small glasses and chill the desserts until ready to serve. Decorate with mixed berries.

yummy hot nut chocolate

Serves 1

Preparation time 5 minutes

Cooking time 5 minutes

300 ml (½ pint) Rich Nut Milk (*see* page 134) or other unsweetened nut milk

2 squares of dairy-free plain chocolate, about 15 g (½ oz), broken into small pieces

¼ teaspoon ground cinnamon, plus extra to serve

maple syrup, honey or soft brown sugar, to taste

fruit, for dunking (optional)

Rich and chocolaty, this is real hot chocolate, none of your powdered stuff! It makes a treat of a drink.

1 Heat the milk and chocolate in a small saucepan over a low heat, stirring, until the chocolate melts. Add the cinnamon and heat through until warm and thick.

2 Add syrup, honey or sugar to taste, then pour into a mug and sprinkle over extra cinnamon. Serve with fresh fruit for dunking, if liked.

fruity popsicles

Makes 6–8

Preparation time 15 minutes, plus cooling and freezing

Cooking time 5 minutes

3 ripe nectarines, halved, stoned and chopped

2 tablespoons icing sugar, plus extra to taste

1 tablespoon water

200 g (7 oz) frozen pitted dark cherries

175 ml (6 fl oz) dairy-free custard (*see* page 139 for homemade)

1 Put the nectarines in a saucepan with the sugar and measurement water, then slowly bring almost to the boil. Reduce the heat and simmer for about 5 minutes, stirring occasionally, until softened. Leave to cool.

2 Put the nectarines in a food processor or blender, add the cherries and custard and blend until smooth and creamy. Add a little extra icing sugar, if liked.

3 Spoon the fruit mixture into 6–8 lolly moulds, depending on their size, and freeze until firm.

strawberry soufflé omelette

Serves 2

Preparation time 15 minutes

Cooking time 5 minutes

2 eggs, separated

2 teaspoons caster sugar

½ teaspoon vanilla extract

1 teaspoon dairy-free spread or coconut oil

125 g (4 oz) strawberries, hulled and halved

large handful of blueberries

icing sugar, for dusting

Cashew Cream (*see* page 140), Coconut Vanilla Cream (*see* page 141) or dairy-free yogurt, to serve

It may come as a surprise to learn that omelettes can be sweet as well as savoury. This one is light as a cloud and topped with lots of fresh strawberries and blueberries.

1 Whisk the egg whites in a large, grease-free bowl until they hold their shape. Gradually add the sugar, whisking well between each addition, until the mixture is stiff and glossy. Whisk in the vanilla extract. Beat the egg yolks, then gently fold them in.

2 Melt the spread or coconut oil in a medium-sized ovenproof frying pan and swirl it to around to coat the base. Tip the frothy egg mixture into the pan and gently spread it out with a spatula, leaving a few peaks and troughs. Cook over a medium-low heat for 2–3 minutes until the base is set and light golden. Place under a preheated hot grill and lightly cook the top until just set.

3 Slide the omelette on to a serving plate and top with the strawberries and blueberries and a dusting of icing sugar. Halve the omelette, then serve with spoonfuls of Cashew Cream, Coconut Vanilla Cream or yogurt.

melon slush

Serves 4–6

**Preparation time 15 minutes,
  plus freezing**

1 kg (2 lb) ripe melon, such as honeydew
  or watermelon

juice of 2 limes

3 tablespoons icing sugar, plus extra
  to taste

strips of lime rind, to decorate (optional)

This fresh fruit slush is super-refreshing on
a hot summer's day.

1 Quarter the melon and remove the seeds. Scoop out the flesh
into a food processor or blender and blend to a coarse purée.

2 Tip into a freezer-proof container with a lid. Stir in the lime
juice and icing sugar, adding extra if liked. Freeze for 2 hours.

3 Remove from the freezer and break up the ice crystals using
a fork. Return to the freezer for 2 hours or until frozen.

4 Remove from the freezer to soften about 20 minutes before
serving. Using a fork, scrape the top of the frozen melon
into loose crystals, then spoon the slush into glasses. Serve
decorated with a few strips of lime rind, if liked.

rhubarb with custard pots

Serves 4

Preparation time 15 minutes, plus infusing

Cooking time 30 minutes

dairy-free spread, for greasing

300 ml (½ pint) unsweetened dairy-free milk

200 ml (7 fl oz) oat cream or other dairy-free cream

1 cinnamon stick

3 large eggs, lightly beaten

50 g (2 oz) caster sugar

1 teaspoon vanilla extract

Rhubarb

200 g (7 oz) rhubarb, sliced

25 g (1 oz) caster sugar

finely grated rind and juice of ½ orange

This classic combination can't be beaten! You may notice that many of the dessert recipes in this book feature vanilla extract and/or spices – there are two good reasons for this: firstly, they taste delicious; and, secondly, it means you don't need to use so much sugar. A double bonus!

1 Lightly grease 4 x 150 ml (¼ pint) pudding basin moulds or large ramekins.

2 Put the milk, cream and cinnamon stick in a small saucepan and heat to almost boiling point, stirring occasionally. Remove the pan from the heat and leave to infuse for 10 minutes.

3 Meanwhile, whisk together the eggs and sugar in a bowl until pale and creamy.

4 When infused, briefly reheat the milk, then strain into the egg mixture, discarding the cinnamon, and stir in the vanilla extract.

5 Pour the custard into the prepared pudding basins and put them in a baking tin. Pour enough just-boiled water into the tin to come two-thirds of the way up the basin sides. Carefully place in a preheated oven, 170°C (340°F), Gas Mark 3½, for 25 minutes or until the custards have set but are still slightly wobbly. Meanwhile, put the rhubarb, sugar and orange rind and juice in a saucepan and heat gently for 8–10 minutes until tender.

6 Remove the custards from the oven and leave to cool slightly, then run a knife around the inside edge of each basin and turn out into serving bowls. Serve with the rhubarb.

chocolate (& avocado) pots

Serves 4

**Preparation time 15 minutes,
plus soaking and chilling**

65 g (2½ oz) ready-to-eat dried dates,
quartered

75 ml (3 fl oz) just-boiled water

1 large avocado, halved, stoned
and peeled

30 g (1 oz) good-quality cocoa powder

1 teaspoon vanilla extract

4 teaspoons maple syrup or honey

100 ml (3½ fl oz) unsweetened almond
milk (*see* page 134 for homemade)
or other dairy-free milk

1 teaspoon coconut oil, melted

4 tablespoons Cashew Cream (*see* page
140) or other dairy-free cream

favourite fruit, to serve

No one will catch on that these indulgent
little chocolate pots contain avocado –
best keep it a secret!

1 Put the dates in a heatproof bowl, cover with the measurement
water and leave to soak for 30 minutes until softened.

2 Put the dates and soaking water in a food processor or
blender, add the avocado, cocoa powder, vanilla extract, maple
syrup, milk and coconut oil and blend until smooth and creamy.

3 Spoon the mixture into 4 small glasses or ramekins and chill
for 30 minutes. Top each with the cashew cream and serve with
your favourite fruit.

apple syrup puddings

Serves 4

Preparation time 15 minutes

Cooking time 30–35 minutes

75 g (3 oz) dairy-free spread, plus extra
for greasing

75 g (3 oz) caster sugar

100 g (3½ oz) self-raising flour

½ teaspoon baking powder

1 teaspoon vanilla extract

2 eggs, lightly beaten

3 tablespoons unsweetened
dairy-free milk

1 unpeeled dessert apple, grated

4 heaped teaspoons golden syrup

warm dairy-free custard (*see* page 139
for homemade), to serve

1 Lightly grease 4 x 150 ml (¼ pint) fluted or regular metal pudding basin moulds.

2 Put the spread, sugar, flour, baking powder, vanilla extract, eggs and milk in a food processor or blender and blend together for 2 minutes until smooth and creamy. Alternatively, place in a bowl and beat together using a hand-held electric mixer. Fold in the apple.

3 Spoon 1 heaped teaspoon of the syrup into each prepared basin, then top with the apple mixture. Transfer the basins to a baking tray and bake in a preheated oven, 180°C (350°F), Gas Mark 4, for 30–35 minutes until risen and golden. Leave to cool for a few minutes, then run a knife around the inside edge of each basin and turn out on to serving plates. Serve with warm custard.

apple & blueberry crisp

Serves 4–6

Preparation time 15 minutes

Cooking time 40 minutes

2 Bramley apples, peeled, cored and cut into bite-sized pieces

40 g (1½ oz) caster sugar

2 tablespoons water

3 handfuls of blueberries or blackberries

dairy-free vanilla ice cream or dairy-free custard (*see* page 139 for homemade), to serve

Topping

50 g (2 oz) plain flour

60 g (2¼ oz) soft light brown sugar

40 g (1½ oz) jumbo oats

40 g (1½ oz) ground almonds

½ teaspoon ground cinnamon

25 g (1 oz) pecan nuts, roughly chopped

75 g (3 oz) coconut oil

This variation on the traditional apple crumble has a lightly spiced crunchy oat, nut and coconut oil topping.

1 Put the apples, caster sugar and measurement water in a saucepan, cover and cook for 6–8 minutes until the apples start to break down. Spoon into a 1.2 litre (2 pint) ovenproof dish and stir in the blueberries or blackberries.

2 Mix together all of the topping ingredients, except the coconut oil, in a bowl. Heat the coconut oil gently in a small saucepan, then leave to cool slightly. Pour into the dry ingredients, then stir until combined and the mixture comes together in small clumps.

3 Spoon the topping on to the fruit and place in a preheated oven, 180°C (350°F), Gas Mark 4, for 30 minutes or until slightly crisp and golden on top. Serve with dairy-free vanilla ice cream or custard.

fruit bun pudding

Serves 6

Preparation time 15 minutes,
plus standing

Cooking time 40–45 minutes

6 dairy-free hot cross buns or other
  fruit buns, split in half

dairy-free spread, for spreading

150 ml (¼ pint) dairy-free cream

300 ml (½ pint) unsweetened
  dairy-free milk

1 teaspoon vanilla extract

1 teaspoon mixed spice

3 eggs

50 g (2 oz) caster sugar, plus extra
  for sprinkling

This dairy-free version of bread-and-butter pudding is made with hot cross buns or fruit buns. You could also add a handful of chopped dried apricots to the pudding and sprinkle pecans over the top.

1 Spread the hot cross buns with spread, then arrange in 2 layers, slightly overlapping and spread side up, in a 1.2 litre (2 pint) ovenproof dish.

2 Put the cream, milk, vanilla extract and mixed spice in a saucepan and bring almost to the boil. Meanwhile, whisk together the eggs and caster sugar in a heatproof bowl. Pour in the cream mixture, whisking continuously, until combined.

3 Pour the custard mixture over the hot cross buns, pressing them down into the liquid. Leave to stand for 10 minutes, then sprinkle over a little extra sugar.

4 Place the dish in a baking tin and pour in enough just-boiled water to come halfway up the sides. Carefully place in a preheated oven, 180°C (350°F), Gas Mark 4, and cook for 35–40 minutes until set and crisp and golden on top.

raspberry popovers

Makes 6

Preparation time 10 minutes, plus standing

Cooking time 25 minutes

75 g (2½ oz) plain flour

pinch of salt

125 ml (4 fl oz) unsweetened almond milk (*see* page 134 for homemade) or other dairy-free milk

1 large egg, lightly beaten

3 teaspoons sunflower oil

To serve

fresh raspberries

maple syrup or honey

Cashew Cream (*see* page 140) or Coconut Vanilla Cream (*see* page 141)

The simplest way to describe these would be a sweet version of the classic Yorkshire pudding – and they are just yummy! As with Yorkshires, you need to get the oil really hot before adding the batter so they rise and become light and fluffy inside.

1 Sift the flour, baking powder and salt into a large bowl and make a well in the centre. Whisk together the milk and egg in a jug, then gradually pour into the dry ingredients, whisking continuously to form a smooth batter. Transfer the batter to a jug and leave to stand for 20 minutes.

2 Divide the oil between a 6-hole muffin tray. Heat in a preheated oven, 220°C (425°F), Gas Mark 7, for 6 minutes until very hot. Carefully remove the tray from the oven and pour in the batter. Return to the oven and cook for 17–20 minutes until risen and golden.

3 Scatter raspberries over each popover, then drizzle with syrup or honey and serve with good spoonfuls of dairy-free cream.

coconut rice pudding

Serves 4

Preparation time 10 minutes

Cooking time 30 minutes

125 g (4 oz) short-grain brown rice

500 ml (17 fl oz) coconut drinking milk
(*see* page 135 for homemade), plus extra
if needed

40 g (1½ oz) caster sugar

½ teaspoon ground cinnamon or crushed
cardamom seeds

1 teaspoon vanilla extract

To serve

Sliced or chopped fresh or dried fruit,
such as mango, banana, pear, dried
apricots, dates or raisins

handful of pecan nuts, toasted and
roughly chopped

Rice pudding, if made in the traditional way,
takes a while to bake. This speedy version
uses short-grain brown rice, but if you can't
find it you could use pudding rice instead.

1 Cook the rice according to the packet instructions until
tender, then drain, if necessary, and return the rice to the pan.

2 Pour the milk into the pan and heat over a medium-low heat
for 10 minutes, stirring continuously and adding a little extra
milk if the mixture looks too dry. Stir in the sugar, cinnamon or
cardamom and vanilla extract and cook for a further 5 minutes
until thick and creamy.

3 Spoon the pudding into 4 bowls and serve topped with fruit
and chopped pecan nuts.

banana melts

Serves 4

Preparation time 10 minutes

4 bananas, sliced

100 g (3½ oz) dairy-free soft cheese

125 g (4 oz) dairy-free yogurt, preferably
unsweetened

1 teaspoon vanilla extract

4 teaspoons light muscovado sugar

Perfect for a weekday pudding, this is quick
and easy to make.

1 Divide the bananas among 4 serving glasses or bowls.

2 Put the soft cheese, yogurt and vanilla extract in a bowl and
beat together until smooth, then spoon over the bananas.

3 Sprinkle 1 teaspoon of the sugar over each serving and wait
for a few minutes for it to melt before serving.

cherry cheesecake brûlées

Serves 4

Preparation time 15 minutes, plus cooling

Cooking time 5 minutes

1 heaped teaspoon cornflour

2 teaspoons water

300 g (10 oz) frozen pitted dark cherries

4 dairy-free digestive biscuits, crushed

125 g (4 oz) dairy-free cream cheese

125 ml (4 fl oz) dairy-free coconut yogurt or other thick dairy-free yogurt

2 heaped teaspoons demerara sugar

A cross between a cheesecake and a crème brûlée, these individual desserts need to be made in advance to allow time for chilling.

1 Mix the cornflour and measurement water to a paste in a cup. Put the cherries in a saucepan with a splash of water and heat until defrosted. Stir in the cornflour paste and cook, stirring, for 2 minutes until thickened. Leave to cool.

2 Divide the crushed digestives among 4 ramekins and top with the cherry mixture.

3 Put the cream cheese and yogurt in a bowl and beat together until smooth and creamy, then spoon over the cherries in an even layer. Sprinkle the sugar over the ramekins and mist the tops with a splash of water (this helps the sugar to caramelize).

4 Transfer the ramekins to a grill pan and place under a preheated hot grill for 2–3 minutes or until the sugar melts and starts to caramelize (keep an eye on them as the sugar can burn easily). Leave to cool, or chill, before serving.

treats &
special occasions

lemon & almond drizzle

Serves 12

Preparation time 15 minutes, plus cooling

Cooking time 45–50 minutes

175 g (6 oz) dairy-free spread, plus extra
  for greasing

175 g (6 oz) caster sugar

3 eggs

175 g (6 oz) self-raising flour

finely grated rind of 2 lemons

1 teaspoon vanilla extract

50 g (2 oz) ground almonds

3 tablespoons lemon juice

Lemon icing

5 tablespoons icing sugar

5–6 teaspoons lemon juice

This moist, lemony Madeira cake is made in a loaf tin, but it also looks pretty baked in mini individual loaf tins or cases.

1 Lightly grease and line the base of a 500 g (1 lb) loaf tin.

2 Beat together the spread and caster sugar in a large bowl until pale and fluffy. Add the eggs, one at a time, beating well between each addition and adding a spoonful of flour if the mixture starts to curdle. Stir in the lemon rind and vanilla extract. Sift in the flour and ground almonds, then fold in the lemon juice.

3 Spoon the mixture into the prepared loaf tin and smooth the top with the back of the spoon. Cook in a preheated oven, 180°C (350°F), Gas Mark 4, for 45–50 minutes until a skewer inserted into the centre comes out clean. Leave to cool in the tin for 5 minutes, then turn out on to a wire rack, remove the baking paper and leave to cool.

4 Make the icing. Sift the icing sugar into a bowl and stir in enough lemon juice to form a soft but not runny icing. Drizzle the icing over the top of the cooled cake and leave to set.

merry berry filo tarts

Makes 8

Preparation time 15 minutes, plus cooling

Cooking time 20 minutes

50 g (2 oz) coconut oil, melted

8 sheets of filo pastry, about 30 x 18 cm (12 x 7 inches) each

1 recipe quantity Coconut Vanilla Cream (*see* page 141)

200 g (7 oz) mixed berries, such as blueberries, blackcurrants, strawberries and raspberries

2 teaspoons icing sugar, for dusting

1 Grease 8 holes of a 12-hole muffin tray with a little of the melted coconut oil.

2 Cut each sheet of filo into 3 x 10 cm (4 inch) squares, to make 24 squares in total; discard the pastry offcuts.

3 Carefully press a square of filo into each prepared hole in the muffin tray and lightly brush with the melted coconut oil. Place a second sheet of filo diagonally on top, brush with more coconut oil, then place a final sheet of filo in each hole to make 8 baskets with a star-shaped top.

4 Cook in a preheated oven, 180°C (350°F), Gas Mark 4, for about 20 minutes or until golden and crisp. Transfer to a wire rack to cool.

5 Spoon the coconut vanilla cream into the filo cups and top with the berries. Dust with icing sugar before serving.

chocolate beetroot brownies

Makes 12

Preparation time 15 minutes, plus cooling

Cooking time 25–30 minutes

150 ml (¼ pint) sunflower oil, plus extra
  for greasing

100 g (3½ oz) dairy-free plain chocolate,
  broken into pieces

3 eggs

200 g (7 oz) caster sugar

100 g (3½ oz) self-raising flour

50 g (2 oz) cocoa powder, plus extra
  to decorate

50 g (2 oz) ground almonds

1 teaspoon baking powder

200 g (7 oz) ready-cooked beetroot
  in natural juice, patted dry and
  coarsely grated

1 teaspoon vanilla extract

1 Grease and line the base of a 20 cm (8 inch) square cake tin.

2 Melt the chocolate in a bowl set over a saucepan of gently simmering water, making sure the bottom of the bowl doesn't touch the water, then leave to cool slightly.

3 Meanwhile, whisk together the eggs and sugar in a large bowl until pale and fluffy. Gradually beat in the oil, flour, cocoa powder, almonds, baking powder, beetroot and vanilla extract, then add the melted chocolate.

4 Pour the mixture into the prepared tin and cook in a preheated oven, 180°C (350°F), Gas Mark 4, for 20–25 minutes until risen and just cooked – it should still be slightly squidgy in the middle. Leave to cool in the tin for 5 minutes, then turn out on to a wire rack and leave to cool. Remove the baking paper and decorate with a light dusting of cocoa powder. Cut into 12 squares before serving.

fruit 'n' nut cookies

Makes 12

Preparation time 15 minutes, plus cooling

Cooking time 18 minutes

75 g (3 oz) ready-to-eat dried apricots

100 g (3½ oz) plain flour

65 g (2½ oz) porridge oats

50 g (2 oz) hazelnuts, chopped

125 g (4 oz) dairy-free spread or coconut oil

75 g (3 oz) soft light brown sugar

2 tablespoons golden syrup

1 Line a baking sheet with nonstick baking paper. Cut the apricots into small pieces. Place the flour, oats, hazelnuts and apricot pieces in a bowl and stir until combined.

2 Put the spread or oil, sugar and syrup in a small saucepan and heat gently, stirring occasionally, until melted. Pour into the dry ingredients and stir to form a soft, chunky dough.

3 Place 12 heaped dessertspoonfuls of dough on the prepared baking sheet, spaced well apart, and flatten the tops slightly. Bake in a preheated oven, 180°C (350°F), Gas Mark 4, for 15 minutes or until light golden. Transfer to a wire rack to cool and crisp up.

peanut butter cookies

Makes 10

Preparation time 15 minutes

Cooking time 17–20 minutes

75 g (3 oz) dairy-free plain chocolate

40 g (1½ oz) unsalted roasted peanuts

50 g (2 oz) peanut butter

50 g (2 oz) dairy-free spread

100 g (3½ oz) soft light brown sugar

1 egg, lightly beaten

100 g (3½ oz) plain flour

½ teaspoon baking powder

pinch of salt

1 Line a baking sheet with nonstick baking paper. Break the chocolate into chunks and roughly chop the roasted peanuts.

2 Beat together the peanut butter, spread and sugar in a large bowl until light and creamy. Beat in the egg, adding a spoonful of the flour if the mixture starts to curdle. Fold in the flour, baking powder and salt, then the chocolate pieces and peanuts.

3 Spoon 10 heaped dessertspoonfuls of the mixture on to the prepared baking sheet and flatten the tops slightly. Place in a preheated oven, 180°C (350°F), Gas Mark 4, for 17–20 minutes until golden but still slightly soft and gooey in the centres. Transfer to a wire rack to cool.

banana muffins with cinnamon frosting

Makes 10

Preparation time 20 minutes, plus cooling and chilling

Cooking time 20–25 minutes

225 g (7½ oz) plain flour

1½ teaspoons baking powder

150 g (5 oz) soft light brown sugar

2 large eggs

4 tablespoons unsweetened dairy-free milk

125 g (4 oz) dairy-free spread or coconut oil, melted and cooled

2 large ripe bananas, mashed

Cinnamon frosting

100 g (3½ oz) dairy-free cream cheese

75 g (3 oz) icing sugar, plus extra to taste

1 teaspoon vanilla extract

1 teaspoon ground cinnamon

1 Line 10 holes of a 12-hole muffin tray with muffin cases.

2 Sift the flour, baking powder and brown sugar into a large bowl. Stir until combined, then make a well in the centre. Beat together the eggs, milk and melted spread or oil in a jug, then pour into the dry ingredients and add the bananas. Using a wooden spoon, gently stir together until just combined.

3 Spoon the mixture into the muffin cases and cook in a preheated oven, 190°C (375°F), Gas Mark 5, for 20–25 minutes or until risen. Transfer to a wire rack to cool.

4 Meanwhile, make the cinnamon frosting. Put the cream cheese, icing sugar, vanilla extract and cinnamon in a bowl and beat together until smooth, thick and creamy, adding a little extra icing sugar to taste, if liked, then chill to firm up. Decorate each muffin with a spoonful of the frosting.

Tips and tricks
The secret to light, moist muffins is to not over-mix the cake batter; it doesn't matter if the ingredients aren't thoroughly combined.

mini strawberry vanilla cheesecakes

Makes 4–6

Preparation time 20 minutes, plus cooling and chilling

Cooking time 30 minutes

40 g (1½ oz) dairy-free spread

65 g (2½ oz) dairy-free digestive biscuits, crushed

15 g (½ oz) ground almonds

250 g (8 oz) strawberries, hulled and halved if large

2 teaspoons icing sugar

Filling

125 ml (4 fl oz) dairy-free yogurt, preferably unsweetened

175 g (6 oz) dairy-free cream cheese

2 tablespoons dairy-free cream

2 egg yolks, beaten

2 tablespoons maple syrup or honey

1 teaspoon vanilla extract

juice of ½ lemon

1½ teaspoons cornflour

A deep muffin tray is the perfect container for these individual cheesecakes, which are just the perfect size for children.

1 Line 4 x 250 ml (8 fl oz) mini cheesecake tins with baking paper. Alternatively line 6 holes of a muffin tin with baking paper by cutting 2 strips and pressing them into the muffin holes, laying one perpendicular to the other to form a cross shape.

2 Melt the spread in a small saucepan, then stir in the crushed biscuits and ground almonds. Divide the mixture evenly among the prepared cheesecake tins and press down to make firm, even bases. Cook in a preheated oven, 180°C (350°F), Gas Mark 4, for 10 minutes until just crisp.

3 Meanwhile, beat together all the filling ingredients in a bowl until smooth and creamy. Spoon the mixture over the biscuit bases and level the tops, then return to the oven for a further 17–20 minutes or until firm and just set. Leave to cool in the tins, then chill for at least 30 minutes.

4 Place the strawberries in a bowl and sprinkle over the icing sugar. Stir together, then leave until the juices start to run.

5 When ready to serve, carefully remove the cheesecakes from the tins on to serving plates. Spoon the strawberries and any juice on top of the cheesecakes.

strawberries & cream birthday cake

Serves 8–10

Preparation time 20 minutes, plus cooling and chilling

Cooking time 35–45 minutes

400 g (13 oz) self-raising flour, plus extra for dusting

1 teaspoon baking powder

½ teaspoon bicarbonate of soda

250 g (8 oz) caster sugar

115 ml (3¾ fl oz) sunflower oil

400 ml (14 fl oz) unsweetened almond milk (*see* page 134 for homemade) or other dairy-free milk

3 tablespoons golden syrup

2 teaspoons vanilla extract

4 tablespoons strawberry jam

Buttercream

200 g (7 oz) dairy-free spread, plus extra for greasing

175 g (6 oz) icing sugar, sifted, plus extra to decorate

1 teaspoon vanilla extract

To decorate

2 handfuls of dairy-free chocolate buttons

200 g (7 oz) strawberries, hulled and halved or quartered depending on size

This simple celebration cake is topped with dairy-free buttercream and chocolate buttons, and fresh strawberries.

1 Grease and flour the sides of 2 x 23 cm (9 inch) loose-bottomed cake tins, then line the bases.

2 Sift the flour, baking powder, bicarbonate of soda and sugar into a large bowl, then stir together. Whisk together the oil, milk, syrup and vanilla extract in a jug, then pour into the dry ingredients and whisk for 2 minutes until thick and creamy.

3 Spoon the mixture into the prepared cake tins and bake in a preheated oven, 180°C (350°F), Gas Mark 4, for 35–45 minutes until risen and cooked through. Leave to cool in the tins for 10 minutes, then turn out on to a wire rack, remove the baking paper and leave to cool completely.

4 Meanwhile, make the buttercream. Beat together all the ingredients in a bowl until thick and creamy, then chill until firm.

5 Spread the jam evenly over 1 cake and top with two-thirds of the buttercream. Top with the remaining cake and spread the remaining buttercream over the top. Decorate the top edge of the cake with chocolate buttons and pile the strawberries in the centre. Dust with extra icing sugar before serving.

easy chocolate cherry cake

Serves 12

Preparation time 15 minutes, plus cooling
  and chilling

Cooking time 45–50 minutes

75 ml (3 fl oz) plus 1 teaspoon sunflower
  oil, plus extra for greasing

225 g (7½ oz) plain flour

225 g (7½ oz) caster sugar

1 teaspoon bicarbonate of soda

½ teaspoon salt

3 tablespoons good-quality cocoa powder

1 teaspoon vanilla extract

1 tablespoon distilled vinegar or white
  vinegar

250 ml (8 fl oz) water

100 g (3½ oz) dried cherries

Chocolate frosting

100 g (3½ oz) dairy-free cream cheese

50 g (2 oz) icing sugar, sifted

1 teaspoon cocoa powder

1 teaspoon vanilla extract

Egg-free, this is one of the easiest cakes to
make and tastes delicious, too.

1 Lightly grease and line a 500 g (1 lb) loaf tin.

2 Sift the flour, caster sugar, bicarbonate of soda, salt and
cocoa powder into a large bowl, then stir until combined. In a
separate bowl, mix together the oil, vanilla extract, vinegar and
measurement water. Pour into the dry ingredients, add the
cherries and stir with a wooden spoon until combined.

3 Pour the mixture into the prepared tin and bake in a preheated
oven, 180°C (350°F), Gas Mark 4, for 45–50 minutes until risen and
a skewer inserted into the centre comes out clean. Leave to cool
in the tin for 5 minutes, then turn out on to a wire rack, remove
the baking paper and leave to cool completely.

4 Put all the frosting ingredients in a bowl and beat together
until smooth and creamy. Chill for 30 minutes to firm up, then
spoon over the cake before serving.

raspberry & caramel trifles

Serves 6

Preparation time 20 minutes, plus cooling and chilling

Cooking time 35 minutes

300 g (10 oz) frozen raspberries, defrosted

500 ml (17 fl oz) dairy-free custard (see page 139 for homemade), cooled

½ recipe quantity Coconut Vanilla Cream (see page 141) or 2 recipe quantities Cashew Cream (see page 140)

½ recipe quantity Dairy-free Caramel Sauce (see page 141) or 25 g (1 oz) dairy-free plain chocolate, grated

Sponge

150 g (5 oz) dairy-free spread, plus extra for greasing

150 g (5 oz) caster sugar

1 teaspoon vanilla extract

150 g (5 oz) self-raising flour

½ teaspoon baking powder

1 large egg, lightly beaten

4 tablespoons unsweetened dairy-free milk

This is a conglomeration of a few recipes in this book, which all come together to make a treat of a pudding – just the thing for a special occasion. The trifle can also be made in a single large serving bowl.

1 Grease and line a 23 cm (9 inch) loose-bottomed cake tin.

2 Beat together all the sponge ingredients in a large bowl for 2 minutes until pale and creamy. Spoon the mixture into the prepared tin and bake in a preheated oven, 180°C (350°F), Gas Mark 4, for 35 minutes or until risen and cooked through. Leave to cool in the tin for 5 minutes, then turn out on to a wire rack, remove the baking paper and leave to cool completely.

3 Break the sponge into pieces and divide between 6 individual dessert glasses. Put the raspberries in a separate bowl and lightly crush with the back of a fork. Spoon over the sponge pieces, then divide the custard between the glasses, spreading it evenly over the top of the crushed raspberries. Spoon over the cream, then drizzle with the caramel sauce or sprinkle over the grated chocolate. Chill for 30 minutes before serving.

peaches & cream pavlovas

Makes 6

Preparation time 15 minutes, plus cooling

Cooking time 30 minutes

3 egg whites

1 teaspoon cornflour

150 g (5 oz) caster sugar

1 recipe quantity Coconut Vanilla Cream (*see* page 141)

3 ripe peaches, halved, stoned and sliced

maple syrup or honey, for drizzling

Make sure the peaches are ripe and juicy when making this pretty summery dessert. In place of the peaches, you could use nectarines, strawberries, raspberries or cherries.

1 Line a large baking sheet with nonstick baking paper and draw 6 x 8.5 cm (3½ inch) circles on to the paper.

2 Using a hand-held electric whisk on a low speed, whisk the egg whites in a large, grease-free bowl for about 2 minutes until foamy, then increase the speed to medium and continue to whisk for 1 minute. Increase the speed to high and whisk until stiff peaks form and the mixture is light and fluffy.

3 Still on a high speed, whisk in the cornflour and then the sugar, a dessertspoonful at a time, until the mixture looks stiff and glossy. (Adding the sugar slowly prevents the meringue weeping when cooked.)

4 Spoon the meringue on to the circles on the baking paper, then make a slight crater in the centre of each one with the back of a spoon. Bake in a preheated oven, 150°C (300°F), Gas Mark 2, for 30 minutes or until the outside of the meringues are crisp and the centres are slightly soft. Turn off the oven and leave the meringues in the oven until cold.

5 Place a large dollop of the coconut vanilla cream on each meringue. Arrange the peaches on top, then add a drizzle of maple syrup or honey and serve.

basics

nut milk

Makes about 500 ml (17 fl oz)

Preparation time 15 minutes,
  plus soaking

100 g (3½ oz) blanched almonds or
  cashew nuts

500 ml (17 fl oz) filtered water

Almonds and cashew nuts both make a creamy, non-dairy milk. This is an excellent everyday milk for drinking, adding to other recipes or pouring over cereal.

1 Put the nuts in a bowl and cover with plenty of cold water. Cover with a plate and leave to soak for 6–8 hours, or overnight.

2 Drain the nuts, discarding the soaking water, and rinse under cold running water. Tip into a food processor or blender with the filtered water and blend on a high speed for about 2 minutes or until the nuts are ground into a fine meal and the water is creamy white.

3 Strain the mixture through a nut milk bag or a muslin-lined sieve, reserving the strained milky liquid in a bowl. Gather up the sides of the bag or the muslin and squeeze to extract as much liquid as possible into the bowl. (The nut meal left in the bag can be used to make the nut cheese on page 33 or stirred into breakfast muesli or porridge.)

4 Pour the strained milk into a lidded container and store in the refrigerator for up to 3 days.

Tips and tricks

For a thicker Rich Nut Milk, follow the recipe above but reduce the filtered water to 250 ml (8 fl oz), and for Nut Cream use 100 ml (3½ fl oz) filtered water – you may need to scrape the nuts down the sides of the food processor or blender and it will take slightly longer to get to a creamy consistency due to the reduced amount of water.

coconut drinking milk

Makes about 400 ml (14 fl oz)

**Preparation time 15 minutes,
plus overnight soaking**

100 g (3½ oz) desiccated coconut,
preferably unsweetened

400 ml (14 fl oz) filtered water

Excellent for pouring over cereal, you can make this non-dairy milk richer and creamier by reducing the amount of filtered water used. After storage, you'll find the cream rises to the surface of the milk – either scrape this off to serve separately or stir until combined again.

1 Put the coconut in a bowl and pour over enough cold water to cover. Stir well, making sure all the coconut is submerged, cover with a plate and leave to soak overnight.

2 Drain the coconut, discarding the soaking water. Tip into a food processor or blender with the filtered water and blend on high speed for 2 minutes or until the coconut has turned to a fine meal and the liquid is creamy white.

3 Strain the coconut mixture through a nut milk bag or a muslin-lined sieve, reserving the strained milky liquid in a bowl. Gather up the sides of the bag or the muslin and squeeze to extract as much liquid as possible into the bowl. (The coconut meal left in the bag can be sprinkled over breakfast cereal or muesli or added to biscuits and cakes.)

4 Pour the strained milk into a lidded container and store in the refrigerator for up to 3 days.

dairy-free raita

Serves 4

Preparation time 10 minutes

4 tablespoons dairy-free cream cheese

100 ml (3½ fl oz) unsweetened
dairy-free milk

1 tablespoon lemon juice

1 garlic clove, crushed

5 cm (2 inch) piece of cucumber,
quartered lengthways, deseeded
and diced

salt and pepper

In place of the usual yogurt, this raita is made with a combination of dairy-free cream cheese and milk, then flavoured with lemon juice, garlic and cucumber. A classic accompaniment to Indian curries, a spoonful will help to cool any spicy dish.

1 Mix together the cream cheese, milk and lemon juice in a serving bowl.

2 Stir in the garlic and cucumber and season with salt and pepper to taste.

dairy-free tzatziki

Serves 4

Preparation time 10 minutes

125 ml (4 fl oz) dairy-free yogurt,
preferably unsweetened

2 tablespoons dairy-free mayonnaise

1 garlic clove, crushed

1–2 tablespoons lemon juice

5 cm (2 inch) piece of cucumber,
quartered lengthways, deseeded
and diced

large handful of mint leaves, chopped

salt and pepper

A dairy-free twist on the Greek classic, this sauce is delicious with grilled meat, fish and roasted vegetables.

1 Mix together the yogurt, mayonnaise, garlic, half the lemon juice, the cucumber and the mint in a serving bowl.

2 Season with salt and pepper to taste, and add more lemon juice, if liked.

tahini dip

Serves 4

Preparation time 10 minutes

100 g (3½ oz) silken tofu

3 tablespoons light tahini

1 garlic clove, crushed

2 tablespoons extra virgin olive oil

juice of 1 lemon

1–2 tablespoons water

handful of mixed herbs, such as oregano, chives, mint and parsley, chopped (optional)

salt and pepper

This creamy dip-cum-sauce makes a nutritious alternative to mayonnaise and is delicious spooned on top of burgers, patties, falafel and pilafs. It can be made with or without the addition of herbs.

1 Put the tofu, tahini, garlic, oil, lemon juice and half the measurement water in a bowl and blend using a stick blender until smooth and creamy, adding the remaining water if necessary – the mixture should have the consistency of mayonnaise.

2 Stir in the herbs, if using, and season with salt and pepper to taste. Store the sauce in an airtight container in the refrigerator for up to 5 days.

dairy-free white sauce

Makes 600 ml (1 pint)

Preparation time 10 minutes

Cooking time 10 minutes

600 ml (1 pint) unsweetened
    dairy-free milk

1 bay leaf

40 g (1½ oz) dairy-free spread

2 heaped tablespoons plain flour

3 tablespoons nutritional yeast flakes

2 teaspoons Dijon mustard

salt and pepper

A dairy-free white sauce is a useful addition to the cook's repertoire. It can be used as a pouring sauce, flavoured with herbs and lemon juice, as a base for a cheesy sauce for pasta and vegetables or in meat, vegetable or fish pies.

1 Put the milk and bay leaf in a small saucepan and heat gently to simmering point.

2 Melt the spread in a separate saucepan, remove from the heat and stir in the flour with a balloon whisk. Return the pan to a low heat and cook the paste for 1–2 minutes, stirring with a wooden spoon until golden.

3 Gradually pour in the warm milk, stirring continuously, then cook for 5–8 minutes or until thickened to a sauce consistency. Stir in the yeast flakes and mustard and season with salt and pepper to taste.

Tips and tricks

To make a dairy-free béchamel sauce, add an onion studded with 6 cloves to the milk and bay leaf in the pan and bring to simmering point, then turn off the heat and leave to infuse for 30 minutes. Remove the onion, then reheat the milk briefly and continue as above, omitting the yeast flakes and reducing the mustard to 1 teaspoon.

dairy-free custard

Makes about 325 ml (11 fl oz)

Preparation time 5 minutes

Cooking time 10 minutes

325 ml (11 fl oz) unsweetened
  dairy-free milk

1 teaspoon vanilla extract

2 large egg yolks

25 g (1 oz) caster sugar

1 heaped teaspoon cornflour

It is possible to buy non-dairy custard in powdered and ready-made form, but you can't beat homemade.

1 Pour the milk and vanilla extract into a saucepan and heat gently to simmering point.

2 Meanwhile, whisk together the egg yolks, sugar and cornflour in a large heatproof bowl until thickened. Gradually pour the warmed milk into the egg mixture, whisking continuously.

3 Return the custard to the pan and heat gently over a very low heat, stirring with a wooden spoon and making sure you get into the corners of the pan, until thickened. Pour into a jug to serve.

Tips and tricks

It's important to heat the milk very slowly over a low heat to prevent the egg scrambling and curdling in the heat of the milk.

cashew cream

Makes about 100 ml (3½ fl oz)

Preparation time 5 minutes, plus soaking

75 g (3 oz) cashew nuts

4 tablespoons cold water

3 tablespoons dairy-free cream

1 teaspoon vanilla extract

1 tablespoon maple syrup or honey

This sweetened, thick cream is a delicious alternative to whipped cream and can be spooned over fruit, pies and crumble – it's particularly good on meringues.

1 Put the cashews in a heatproof bowl and cover with just-boiled water. Leave to soak for 1 hour.

2 Drain the nuts, discarding the soaking liquid. Tip into a food processor or blender, add the measurement water and blend until smooth and creamy, scraping down the sides of the jug if necessary. Alternatively, blend together using a stick blender.

3 Stir in the cream, vanilla extract and maple syrup or honey before serving.

dairy-free caramel sauce

Serves 6
Preparation time 5 minutes
Cooking time 10 minutes

75 g (3 oz) golden syrup
3 tablespoons soft light brown sugar
40 g (1½ oz) dairy-free spread
125 ml (4 fl oz) dairy-free cream

This golden sauce can be spooned over dairy-free ice cream or yogurt, or fruit, and will keep in the refrigerator for a short time.

1 Place the golden syrup, sugar and spread in a small saucepan and bring slowly to the boil. Reduce the heat to low and cook for 5–8 minutes, stirring occasionally, until thickened to a syrupy consistency.

2 Remove from the heat and stir in the cream. Leave to cool and thicken. Store in a sealable jar in the refrigerator for up to 5 days.

coconut vanilla cream

Makes about 150 ml (¼ pint)
Preparation time 5 minutes, plus chilling

400 ml (14 fl oz) can coconut milk
1 teaspoon vanilla extract
1 tablespoon icing sugar, sifted

Rich and indulgent, this whipped cream is a great replacement for thick double cream.

1 Place the can of coconut milk in the refrigerator for about 2 hours until chilled.

2 Open the can and scoop out the thick coconut cream on the top, leaving the thin coconut water at the bottom (the coconut water can be stored in the refrigerator for about 3 days, or frozen, for use in another recipe). Place about 150 ml (¼ pint) of the thick coconut cream in a bowl.

3 Add the vanilla extract and icing sugar and whip until smooth.

index

acknowledgements

Publisher's credits

Octopus Publishing Group would like to thank all the children featured in this book:
Quentin Deborne, De'shane Fringpone, Florence Kegg, Isabelle Kegg, Nelly Kegg, Celia
Leon, Timeo Leon, Finn May, Dora McHardy, Beatrice Offiler, Fañch Parker and Miri Tobisawa.

Picture credits

Special photography by Ian Wallace.
Other photography:
Fotolia Tombaky 4 background (used throughout).
Octopus Publishing Group William Shaw 16.

Commissioning Editor: **Sarah Ford**
Senior Editor: **Leanne Bryan**
Art Director: **Tracy Killick at Tracy Killick Art Direction and Design**
Design Manager: **Jaz Bahra**
Photographer: **Ian Wallace**
Home economist and stylist: **Louise Pickford**
Picture Library Manager: **Jennifer Veall**
Assistant Production Manager: **John Casey**